TAFF
REF

3   D0969512

WORKPLACE LEARNING & LEADERSHIP

ALA Editions purchases fund advocacy,
awareness, and accreditation programs
for library professionals worldwide.

WORKPLACE LEARNING & LEADERSHIP

A **HANDBOOK** FOR LIBRARY AND NONPROFIT TRAINERS

LORI REED and
PAUL SIGNORELLI

AMERICAN LIBRARY ASSOCIATION

CHICAGO   2011

Lori Reed is the learning and development coordinator for the Charlotte Mecklenburg Library, where she plans and oversees the learning and development of a diverse group of staff at twenty libraries. With more than fifteen years of experience in the workplace learning and development field, Lori is a North Carolina Master Trainer, a certified Synchronous Learning Expert, and was named a 2009 *Library Journal* "Mover and Shaker."

Paul Signorelli is a San Francisco–based writer, trainer, presenter, and consultant who has held a variety of leadership positions. He served as director, Volunteer Services and Staff Training, for the San Francisco Public Library system; is active in the American Society for Training and Development and the American Library Association; and writes for a variety of online and print publications. He can be reached at paul@paulsignorelli.com.

© 2011 by the American Library Association. Any claim of copyright is subject to applicable limitations and exceptions, such as rights of fair use and library copying pursuant to Sections 107 and 108 of the U.S. Copyright Act. No copyright is claimed in content that is in the public domain, such as works of the U.S. government.

Printed in the United States of America

15   14   13   12   11   5   4   3   2   1

While extensive effort has gone into ensuring the reliability of the information in this book, the publisher makes no warranty, express or implied, with respect to the material contained herein.

ISBN: 978–0–8389–1082–5

Library of Congress Cataloging-in-Publication Data
Reed, Lori, 1972–
    Workplace learning and leadership : a handbook for library and nonprofit trainers / Lori Reed, Paul Signorelli.
        p.   cm.
    Includes bibliographical references and index.
    ISBN 978-0-8389-1082-5 (alk. paper)
    1. Library employees—In-service training—United States. 2. Librarians—In-service training—United States. 3. Nonprofit organizations—Employees—In-service training—United States. 4. Employee training personnel. 5. Career development. 6. Organizational learning. I. Signorelli, Paul. II. Title.
    Z668.5.R44 2011
    020.71'55—dc22   2011011670

Cover design by Casey Bayer.
Text design in Minion Pro and Din by Karen Sheets de Gracia.

♾ This paper meets the requirements of ANSI/NISO Z39.48–1992 (Permanence of Paper).

ALA Editions also publishes its books in a variety of electronic formats. For more information, visit the ALA Store at www.alastore.ala.org and select eEditions.

To

Peter Bromberg, Kimberly Bolan Cullin,
and Janie Hermann,
who opened doors;

Christopher Rhodes,
who sustained us with encouragement;

and

Pat Carterette and Robert Zimmerman,
who left before they had a chance
to read this

CONTENTS

CONTENTS

FOREWORD

On behalf of the authors Lori Reed and Paul Signorelli, thank you for picking up this copy of *Workplace Learning and Leadership*. So, why should you add this book to your professional or personal collection?

Well, I have been fortunate to know both of the authors professionally and personally and I am very excited about this book you have in your hand. I am and you will be similarly impressed with the variety and knowledge they were able to extract from a broad array of library learning leaders. Thanks in no small part to Lori and Paul's interviewing skills, these leaders readily shared valuable and practical skills and techniques that have worked and not worked for them in their organizations' training environment.

This book is written from the perspective of the training professional working primarily in public libraries within the United States; however, the knowledge that fills these pages will help anyone who is involved in training, coaching, mentoring, or encouraging staff and the public in any type of organization in any locale. The insights and skills discussed in the book are also readily applicable in any particular employment or training situation.

Are you a new or aspiring trainer and want to know some secrets of successful trainers? Well, you are in luck since many successful trainers were interviewed for this book and provide practical skills and insights from their personal training experience to help someone new to the world of training and learning opportunity development.

Are you the person who directly or indirectly supervises a trainer and would like to know how to support your trainer's work within the framework of a successful organization? You can see how other trainers use post learning opportunity evaluation and continual organizational backing to support the learning objectives during the formal training session, reinforce the skills after the session, and have their training/learning staff heavily involved in organizational decision making processes.

Are you a working trainer in need of some assistance with evaluation? Do you need assistance with learner support? Do you want some pointers on how to make organizational learning a key player at your organization's planning table?

Each of these issues is covered in a concise, clearly written chapter brimming with "how we did what we did" tips, suggestions, and a cautionary tale or two.

Like all good trainers, Lori and Paul have written this book so that it is adaptable to your use and needs. This book would be equally effective used as individual chapters for personal or professional exploration or as an entire book devoured in one or two readings covering the entire subject of *Workplace Learning and Leadership*.

The first chapter, "In the Beginning," will be of interest to both new and not so new trainers and administrators. It is filled with descriptions of how the professionals interviewed in the book fell into training, highlighting that there is no one path to becoming a trainer. Since it is rare for a school to offer a "trainer" track of coursework, trainers come from innumerable fields and accidentally discover their natural gift to convey valuable information effectively and efficiently.

Chapter 2, "Collaboration: Creating a Community of Learning," builds on Chapter 1 and focuses on two issues relevant to any trainer. The chapter's first focus is all about creating your own personal learning space in order to collaborate with fellow trainers as a proven method for improving your skill set. The second focus is on developing your organization's community of learning to support your learning opportunities.

Chapter 3, "Trainers as Internal Consultants and Facilitators of Change," discusses the trainer's role in organizational development and problem solving. Trainers have too often overlooked skills to offer their organization. First is the skill to quickly identify effective training for both individuals and organizational groups. The second skill, equally as critical to organizational success and health, is to quickly diagnose whether a personnel problem is a training issue or an issue better resolved via mentoring, formal discipline, or other human resources management methods.

Chapter 4, "Preparing to Deliver: From Initial Idea to Moment of Delivery," discusses the full gamut of learning opportunity session planning. This cycle starts with the initial development of learning objectives, to the session planning and promotion, Adult Learning Theory, and session delivery. It concludes with post learning opportunity evaluation. This chapter would be most beneficial to the new trainer looking for specific best practices of successful trainers for developing effective and appropriate learning opportunities.

Chapter 5, "In the Middle: Trainers as Leaders in the Classroom," builds and refines Chapter 4's themes by focusing on techniques that work for successful learning opportunity delivery that both supports your initial learning objectives and resonates with your trainees. Methods include the use of intense preparation, humor, and flexibility to ensure you have delivered a successful and memorable (for the right reasons) learning opportunity.

Chapter 6, "When Learning Happens: Supporting Learners after Class," discusses the application of the lessons learned during the learning opportunity and how successful trainers and their organizations support the critical application and retention of material covered in the session. Organizationally unsupported learning opportunities waste the time and talents of everyone involved in developing, delivering, and participating in any learning opportunity.

Chapter 7, "Learning from Success and Failure: The Importance of Effective Evaluations," discusses evaluation both in the learning opportunity setting and post learning opportunity when learners have had a chance to return to their everyday reality and incorporate the lessons into their individual, team, and organizational workflows and processes. This chapter emphasizes the need for evaluating both the short- and long-term effectiveness of the presenters, objectives, and learning materials; it also explores how doing so can make for increased effectiveness of your delivered learning opportunities.

Chapter 8, "Master Trainers, Master Learners: Training the Trainers," focuses on the qualities of a successful future trainer and the power of formal and informal train-the-trainer programs from across the country.

The final chapter, "The End is the Beginning: Leadership and Learning in an Onsite-Online World," reflects on the lessons learned by the trainers interviewed during the course of writing the book and peers into the future world of virtual and blended learning opportunities. Following this last chapter is a list of selected resources which I hope find a home on your bookshelf next to *Workplace Learning and Leadership*.

I have full confidence that Paul and Lori will show you the need for trainers to become the best "trainer-teacher-leaders" they can be. To support their statements and conclusions, they describe and demonstrate tested, proven skills, ideas, and resources that you can use to help you and your organization reach your ultimate potential.

I truly hope that you learn as much as I did from reading this book. Prepare for a great learning journey!

Maurice Coleman
Host/Producer, *T Is for Training*
Library Training Podcast

ACKNOWLEDGMENTS

As readers, we admire the writers who inspire and entertain us. As writers, we want to recognize the fact that writers never finish books unaided.

Former *American Libraries* editor and publisher Leonard Kniffel provided the original playing field for this book by publishing our short article—"Are You Following Me?"—which led us down the path of exploring the important roles trainers play as leaders within their own organizations. American Library Association (ALA) colleagues Peter Bromberg, Kimberly Bolan Cullin, and Janie Hermann, during a long weekend at a conference, helped us see the potential for expanding the article into a book and led us, less than a week later, to the acquisitions editor—Christopher Rhodes—who greeted us with a level of encouragement and enthusiasm that never waned.

Our ALA Learning Round Table colleagues and the others ultimately gave up hours of their time to provide material via interviews that helped shape this book, confirmed what we knew, and brought our attention to much that we should have known but didn't. You'll find them quoted throughout this book, and we want to thank them here for all their magnificent contributions: Peter Bromberg (yes, his much valued fingerprints are all over this book), Helene Blowers, Char Booth, Maurice Coleman, Janet Hildebrand, Raye Oldham, Jason Puckett, Sandra Smith, Jay Turner, Rachel Vacek, Catherine Vaughn, Pat Wagner, and Louise Whitaker. We congratulate Char on her new position at the Claremont Colleges, and Janet on her retirement, both of which came about during the production of this book. We also want to acknowledge the dozens of colleagues from our own communities of learning—the ALA Learning Round Table and its first-rate group of bloggers; the ASTD (American Society for Training & Development) Mt. Diablo Chapter and National Advisors for Chapters; Infopeople; LE@D; the State Library of North Carolina Master Trainer program; and T is for Training—as well as from the Charlotte Mecklenburg, Contra Costa County, and San Francisco public library systems for providing examples of what we have documented in this book.

Staff at ALA Publishing has been a godsend, starting with Christopher Rhodes and including Casey Bayer, Rob Christopher, Jill Davis, Jenni Fry, Megan O'Neill, Dianne Rooney, and John Thomas.

ACKNOWLEDGMENTS

At a very personal level, we want to acknowledge our incredible debt to our spouses and our families for their patience as we disappeared for countless hours to pursue the dream of putting this book in your hands. Thanks to all of them and anyone else we've inadvertently overlooked.

1

IN THE BEGINNING
GETTING TO THE TABLE

Trainers can be the life blood of an organization. They control the information being disseminated during sessions. They hold more power than they may realize.

—Catherine Vaughn, Continuing Education
Coordinator, Lee County Library System

This is an exciting time for those involved in workplace learning and performance (training) programs for libraries and nonprofit organizations—a group much larger than it initially appears to be. The number and rate of changes occurring around the world, the insatiable need for accurate information combined with a torrential overload of resources, and the need for continual learning just so we can remain professionally and intellectually afloat demand creativity and innovation. We struggle with challenges as simple as learning how to operate the latest tech toy we have purchased (or which our employers have purchased for us) and as complex as how to help our customers use even a fraction of the numerous resources and tools we provide.

A minor revolution is under way: "trainers" are increasingly recognizing themselves as "trainer-teacher-learners"—hardly a new role, but one that has not frequently been acknowledged—and they are increasingly finding that their roles require them to step forward as leaders within their organizations.

As if this were not enough to keep all of us busy for the rest of our lifetimes, we are also recognizing that lines are quickly blurring between what could be referred to as "formal" and "informal" trainers, or, as Peter Bromberg, assistant director for the Princeton (New Jersey) Public Library, calls them, "Trainers with a capital T" as opposed to "trainers."

Librarians have long known that library members and guests do not differentiate between "librarians" and other staff members when they are in need of help; if you are working in a library, you are a "librarian" regardless of whether you have the graduate-level degree many librarians have earned. In the same way, employees in libraries and nonprofit organizations are increasingly recognizing that they do not need the word "trainer" in their job titles or on their staff identification badges for their customers to seek that level of assistance from them. In a knowledge-based service culture, almost everyone within a library or nonprofit organization is a trainer-teacher-learner, and anyone who has not noticed that everyone from the chief executive officer to the well-trained and personable custodian has a role to play in this field is not paying attention.

When we are in libraries and notice—as the two of us have—that members of custodial staff as well as library pages, library assistants, members of human resources staff, security guards, and many others help library members and guests find or learn how to find what they need, we know we are in a first-rate organization where collaboration and workplace learning and performance are valued and of value. When we see staff in libraries and nonprofits helping clients learn how to fill out forms on paper and online, we know that training-teaching-learning is important in these organizations, and when we see these elements in place, we know enough to seek out the leaders who make this seamless service possible.

None of this is meant to imply that every staff member has exactly the same set or level of skills and abilities to serve as a trainer-teacher-learner. What it does acknowledge is that each member of a well-functioning library or nonprofit organization either knows enough to provide what the member, guest, or client needs or knows how to lead that person to a colleague who can help meet unfilled needs. The act of leading the person in need to the person able to fill that need is an act of training in itself; it helps our customers learn yet another part of how to navigate the organizations we serve so that those organizations can serve our clients effectively.

The need for everyone to play a role in training-teaching-learning has been embraced more quickly and completely by staff in academic libraries than it has by our colleagues in public libraries, but significant numbers of public library staff are quickly catching up as they take on formal roles in settings as varied as one- or two-hour workshops for library users and one-on-one appointments with librarians through programs designed to meet individual needs at an extremely focused level.

Part of what appears to be making this happen within the most effective libraries and nonprofit organizations is the willingness of workplace learning and performance professionals to act as leaders and the equally important willingness of library and nonprofit administrators to welcome them to the leadership table by including them as members of administrative teams and other high-level committees that plan and implement programs. As management consultant and trainer Pat Wagner notes, the strongest learning cultures exist in those organizations where directors not only support training but also participate alongside members of staff in learning opportunities. They understand what is being offered, understand that their presence encourages others to take training and learning seriously, and gain a perspective not available to those who are disengaged from what is happening within their organizations' learning programs.

Trainers as leaders are the ones who are part of the strategic planning committees; the ones who are presenters at all-staff meetings; and the ones who play the role of internal consultant to assist in implementation of organizations' mission, vision, and value statements. Best of all, they are doing all of this as part of high-functioning, well-trained collaborative teams rather than sitting behind a desk and resting on their laurels.

Bromberg himself was deeply involved in a variety of educational and workplace learning projects in his previous positions before assuming his current leadership at the Princeton Public Library. Contra Costa County (California) deputy county librarian Janet Hildebrand has held a variety of administrative positions while also devoting significant amounts of time and effort to workplace learning and performance projects within the library system she serves and in a regional library training consortium. Louise Whitaker, training coordinator for the Pioneer Library System (Oklahoma), has attended the Public Library Association's Planning for Results Boot Camp, designed to provide staff with management training and skills they did not acquire while earning their MLS or MLIS degrees; she is also actively involved in shaping the PLS Academy, the Pioneer Library System's formal training program, as it develops new content for online tutorials. "What I'm doing is I'm looking around and identifying other capable people and using their skills, helping them grow in a different direction," Whitaker says. "That's part of what a leader does: helps grow other people."

These effective trainer-teacher-learners as leaders are the ones who do not have or give themselves the luxury of looking back with pride at their accomplishments; they are too busily and completely engaged in working with others to create the next successes, and they seem to feed upon success to create yet more success, as becomes obvious from the examples provided throughout this book.

DEFINING TRAINING IN AN EVOLVING FIELD

Discussing leadership and training provides some interesting challenges from the moment the conversation begins. Either term, or a combination of the two terms, produces hundreds of millions of results in an unfocused keyword search of the Internet. The term *leadership* is unambiguous, commonly used, and leads to a significant number of resources when used as a subject-search term in a library catalog. The word *training*, on the other hand, represents a field with a rapidly evolving series of terms.

Although *training* seems to provide common ground for general discussions, those involved in delivering the goods in the workplace use a variety of terms including *training, staff development, career development,* and *occupational training*. The American Society for Training and Development (ASTD) is currently promoting the phrase *workplace learning and performance*. A subject search of library catalogs on *employees, training of,* drawing from the Library of Congress subject heading, consistently produces a larger number of useful results than the other terms do.

The titles given to those in charge of workplace learning and performance programs in libraries and nonprofit organizations reflect the lack of standard terminology in the field. They include, but are far from limited to, director, volunteer services and staff training; training coordinator; training and development manager; training manager; training officer; chief learning officer; learning and development coordinator; staff development and training coordinator; staff development librarian; staff development manager; continuing education coordinator; learning manager; and organizational development manager.

"I dislike the term trainer," Lee County (Florida) Library System continuing education coordinator Catherine Vaughn admits in terms we have heard from others:

> We aren't working with dogs, you know. My title was training coordinator, and when I had a chance to change it to CE coordinator, I did. . . . I think, as our titles evolve, it helps to create an effective program. The title should reflect what is happening, what we are actually doing. Our job is to assist others to be the best they can be. I offer and create sessions geared towards continuing a person's lifetime of education. Trainer just sounds dead-end. Continuing education, staff development, etc. open up possibilities.

Peter Bromberg, when prompted to explore differences between training and teaching, initially quipped, "If I thought about it, I might see a difference, but that would be five minutes of my life I would never get back. And the payoff would be . . . ?" Less than five minutes later, he admitted, "Damn, now you have me thinking about it," and mused over the differences between potty training, training a dog, and training firefighters as opposed to attempting to "train someone in, say, communication." Teaching, he suggests, "seems broader: it encompasses training but could apply less to the creation of an observable skill-based behavior and more to a shift in thought, attitude, or understanding."

Denver Public Library's Sandra Smith also acknowledges the evolving language used in workplace learning and performance and suggests that the title *learning and development manager* might better reflect the way the library is moving—in fact, while we were writing this book, Smith's title did change to reflect her preference. She tells us:

> My thought is that [the title *learning and development manager*] is more familiar in concept of what [the job] is. Learning versus training: one is very familiar in people's experiences, as opposed to training, which sounds required and regimented. Its broader umbrella of experiences is more representative of how learning happens and needs to happen in today's workplace—broader opportunities, flexible in content and logistics, and strategic to operations. So I think that we as trainers can benefit from positioning ourselves in title and in practice as more encompassing in what we can do for staff and the workplace.

"It may be superficial in tone, but it's true that perception is reality in the world and we need to remember that as we strive to make significant contributions to our organizations," she explains.

Many libraries—particularly small and mid-sized systems—do not have formal workplace learning and performance programs or any individual formally designated to organize this sort of program. Others, including the San Francisco Public Library system, actually had more formal training and orientation programs in place for volunteers before formally organizing similar efforts for staff.

The Denver Public Library system, Smith tells us, has a far longer tradition of effort in this field:

> Here at DPL, staff training has been a focus from day one, in 1889, when the library was created. Our first city librarian was John Cotton Dana, and he was the first training manager as he taught classes to his small staff immediately. Later on, another of our city librarians founded the University of Denver Librarianship program. There has been a valuable history of the importance of staff learning throughout

over 120 years, with numerous dedicated training managers and staff contributing. . . . I believe that current trainers, here at DPL and otherwise, do follow a long, valuable line of dedicated librarians and others who believe that a knowledgeable staff is essential to individual libraries as well as to the success of the profession as a whole.

Louise Whitaker, at Pioneer Library System, sees training-teaching-learning as a theme that runs through much of what she does each day with many whom she encounters: "You're sharing your experiences. Not only are you telling them how to do something—'these are some tips'—it can lead into other areas." While attending a workplace meeting, for example, she heard a colleague comment about wanting to know how to access e-mail from home more effectively. Whitaker offered a couple of immediate suggestions and, when the meeting was over, showed her colleague how to make the changes necessary to complete the process—a learning style she frequently employs.

HOW TRAINER-TEACHER-LEARNERS ARE MADE

In the following sections, we see how these workplace learning and performance leaders arrived in the leadership positions they currently hold.

"I fell into it," Louise Whitaker bluntly admits. "I was the information services manager, so I was used to just training my new staff and working with customers. When they wanted to expand the training program at the library system, they asked me to step into that role."

With no formal preparation for a workplace learning and performance position, Whitaker read books and articles, but she found that some of the journals she was exploring were "totally useless." She, like many of her colleagues in similar positions, has learned while meeting the requirements of her job. She engages in searches of professional publications and is continuing to build a collection of workplace learning and performance materials for library employees: "I'm responsible for overseeing that, so I'm constantly on the lookout for new materials—anything that might be of interest to staff: storytelling, readers' advisory, performance evaluation, ethics—anything that staff needs."

She has at least one other thing in common with many of the best trainer-teacher-learners as leaders whom we have met: "I feel very inadequate sometimes," she admits, and she continues to educate herself while helping others.

Gwinnett County (Georgia) Public Library training manager Jay Turner also came to his position in workplace learning and performance with no formal training. He had, however, held what he calls a "hybrid position" in which his time was divided between serving as a library associate in a branch and serving as an assistant within the library training department. "It was that position that provided me with the foundation I needed to become a successful trainer," he reports. "My training manager at the time coached me in all aspects of learning and performance development, even though I was just an associate. Perhaps he saw potential in me that I did not at that time. . . . My undergrad degree is in public relations, and portions of that educational experience contribute to my success in presenting."

Peter Bromberg's exploration of workplace learning and performance easily has been as circuitous. Opting out of a Master of Education program at the last minute, he switched, instead, to library science studies and, while earning his degree, was a substitute teacher in a local high school and junior high school. He also served as a trainer for the *Princeton Review*—an experience he compares to "doing Kabuki Theater. If a *Princeton Review* trainer clears his throat or gets a paper cut, it's in the script."

Attending the New Jersey Train-the-Trainer program, a three-day intensive master trainer program, helped him make the transition from thinking of himself as a "trainer" to thinking of himself as a "Trainer," he says. "That experience gave me a much more structured foundation for understanding training—how to develop a lesson plan, sequence content, respect adult learning principles, do assessment, etc."

Bromberg, like many others interviewed for this book, has also been active in professional organizations including the ALA's Learning Round Table (formerly CLENERT, the Continuing Library Education Network and Exchange Round Table). As a former board member and contributor to the Round Table's blog, *ALA Learning,* he has learned from and taught many of his colleagues how to be more effective in workplace learning and performance.

Learning on the job has also served Janet Hildebrand well with the Contra Costa County Library system. With no formal training "other than being a supervisor for many years," she has served in a variety of positions, including the organization's primary workplace learning and performance advisor:

> I was ready to move on to a new challenge after [serving as] community library manager and applied for central library manager, which came with the responsibility of coordinating new employee training for all new public services staff and designing and implementing the training plan for any system-wide rollout of training for all staff. . . . I love and have always loved watching people grow and be excited by what they

realize they can do that they didn't know they could do, and I've always put in time thinking how to help individuals realize this and grow in their performance, so this didn't seem like a radical step from what I'd always done as a supervisor.

Hildebrand also credits the support of a first-rate supervisor—former Contra Costa County Library director Anne Cain—for much of the success she and the library training program have had and for supporting a model that in turn supports the development of other leaders within the organization:

> I am so lucky to work with a director who understands in her bones that the way you get people to change is to prepare them for the changes. By training them first, you can lead them into change. By training them first and then asking, you will have excited new learners leap ahead and the new leaders showing the more timid responders that it's OK and that the ones in front are having all the fun and it would be OK to go next.

Hildebrand's continuing education has included involvement in a San Francisco Bay area regional training consortium—the Pacific Library Partnership Staff Development Committee (formerly the Library Staff Development Committee of the Greater Bay Area)—as one of several members planning annual "future of libraries" conferences for the group's constituents and providing learning opportunities for members of library support staff in the region.

Denver Public's Sandra Smith followed a similar career path. After earning her MLS from the University of Michigan, she accepted a position as a librarian with Hennepin County (Minnesota) Library. One of her first duties was to create a library orientation program for the public, and she soon "took on the role of training and orienting and support for new librarians at HCL, in part because I work hard and make things happen, but also because I love interacting with people and talk easily with them."

She later developed a system-wide orientation training for new librarians while serving as a branch manager; then moved to Denver Public as a librarian interested in continuing with staff development; subsequently let her new colleagues know of her interest; and, when the training manager retired, accepted an offer to become interim training manager. Smith has continued to develop her skills through two year-long programs that lead to an organization development certificate and a training certificate from the Mountain States Employers Council.

Catherine Vaughn confirms the pattern of learning "from the ground up." With no formal preparation, "I learned what worked and didn't work by trial and error in some cases," she says. "I did, however, bring my experience as an instructor with me when I was a manager in a large department store. That was also 'by default.' I related positively with people and was good at certain tasks, so they asked me to teach new people coming in. I was a selling service manager, so I taught people how to run the registers and techniques for selling, greeting, etc."

Although many of us acknowledge having learned much of what we know on the job, we also have found a variety of resources tremendously helpful. Master trainer programs such as those run by the State Library of North Carolina, the New Jersey State Library, and Infopeople in California (see chapter 8) have provided thorough grounding in all aspects of the skills needed to oversee library workplace learning and performance programs while also introducing participants to colleagues who will serve as resources for members of the cohorts as well as for the library systems they serve.

Another resource cited by a few workplace learning and performance professionals for this book is the Bob Pike Group's monthly "Creative Training Techniques Newsletter," and many of us also benefit tremendously from our affiliation with ALA's Learning Round Table as well as from our active participation in local chapters of ASTD and our membership in the national society. We also find ALA and ASTD publications to be extremely helpful, although many of us acknowledge that we never seem to find enough time to take full advantage of what those publications offer.

The T is for Training group formed by Maurice Coleman, technical trainer for the Harford County (Maryland) Public Library, has also become a cherished resource for library trainers and has a steady following of "usual suspects," including the two of us.

INITIATIVE, VISIBILITY, AND ACCESSIBILITY

One element that is already obvious from Sandra Smith's comments about working hard to "make things happen" is that trainers who serve as leaders show a lot of initiative with the support of their organizations' directors, supervisors, and managers.

Jay Turner managed to move Gwinnett County Public Library from a combination of 90 percent face-to-face and 10 percent e-learning to a mix of 75 percent e-learning and 25 percent face-to-face in a one-year period. Smith worked with colleagues at Denver Public to begin rolling out the comprehensive Employee Learning and Growth Program in 2009 so the program would serve as "a systemic process for DPL's growth as a learning organization." Peter Bromberg has been an active participant in the continuing success of ALA's Emerging Leader program, which began in 2007 as an initiative of Leslie Burger, a past president of the Association. Janet Hildebrand continues to support a peer trainer program that has been the learning model for the Contra Costa County Library system for at least fifteen years. Catherine Vaughn approached members of library administration with the idea of forming a task force to find ways of making more library users aware of the organization's electronic resources; the result was a "librarian's toolbox" program through which databases are featured in two-month increments throughout a one-year period to increase usage, and she has been able to document successes in the continuing program. Pat Wagner provides assistance to libraries throughout the United States and Canada through her leadership, management, and personnel workshops and by writing and producing e-learning through the University of North Texas LE@D (Lifelong Education @ Desktop) program. Louise Whitaker helps develop system-wide goals for the Pioneer Library system, makes reports to the library administrative council, and goes to branches to provide onsite training: "I don't sit back and wait," she notes. "I enjoy getting out and doing things."

The willingness to be visible and accessible is a common trait among those workplace learning and performance leaders. Our colleagues know they can come to us with questions and suggestions for programs that will help them in their day-to-day work. They know they can rely on us to help meet the challenges of the workplace. They know we will do our best to provide the broadest possible access to learning opportunities. Best of all, they know where they can find us and they have come to realize that we are every bit as interested in learning as they are. The result is that formal and informal collaborations create a sense of what is possible rather than a sense that organizational barriers are too powerful to overcome.

SUCCESS WITH LIMITED RESOURCES

One of the more noteworthy achievements of workplace learning and performance professionals who serve as leaders is their ability to succeed with limited resources. Although funding for their programs tends to be more consistent and generous than that provided in organizations where learning is not driven by that level of leadership, it still falls far short of what is common in corporate programs.

Formal staffing is also deceptively small—generally one full-time program coordinator and, in the best of the situations we have seen, a second part- or full-time member of staff to handle administrative details. This, however, hides the level of creativity some display in pulling together an informal group that serves as program faculty.

Learning opportunities at Gwinnett County Public Library are provided by a group of ten to twelve staff members chosen through a competitive process to serve as the library's training team. Those who have a Librarian I designation—two in each of the system's fourteen branches—also serve as training liaisons. The liaisons "are empowered to deliver training based off of approved existing material," Jay Turner explains. "We hold a train-the-trainer workshop to help them identify needs at their branches and present/facilitate for small groups. The L-1s also report back to me any organized on-the-job training they conducted in their branches during any given month. This allows me to stay in tune with what they are doing and, more importantly, to be on the look-out for recurring areas of need that might need addressing from my end."

Contra Costa County Library uses the well-developed peer trainer model that draws large numbers of staff in as part of the training-teaching-learning team. Groups include those involved in new employee training, technology training, and a variety of other continuing programs. As Janet Hildebrand explains it,

> We have a set group of trainers for new employee training [a program that extends over a four-week period] until those trainers start to ask to be replaced, and we phase in new trainers who are carefully recommended, recruited, and groomed as cotrainers and then trainers. We also have various computer-training projects for all staff, and every location and department at this point has a computer competency peer trainer that is their representative for these roll-outs. We also use youth services librarians and one library specialist to train staff in how to conduct successful storytimes for preschoolers, toddlers, and infants. . . . These can all be separate pools, so many staff have opportunities to participate in this experience of teaching and coaching others, and in the culture of our organization it is an honor to be asked, and staff express great pleasure in the experience.

Sandra Smith, at Denver Public, works with one full-time administrative assistant, a training committee she created, and "many staff who assist in the learning program due to my focus on staff-driven and shared knowledge."

Lee County Library System has a combination of training staff, librarians, outside resources, other government or county employees, online resources, web conferencing, and other resources to "enhance our instructional methods to appeal to all learning styles," Catherine Vaughn says. "I do a large number of sessions face-to-face or online. We have also turned to our reference librarians as instructors who specialize in certain subject areas. It is becoming a team effort due to dwindling resources or time and money."

The Charlotte Mecklenburg (North Carolina) Library has one full-time learning and development coordinator and another staff person in the human resources department who coordinates and conducts training for managers and supervisors. Additionally, there is a recently created Learning Council with representatives from all areas of the library serving as advisors and champions of learning.

The San Francisco Public Library staff training program has operated in a similar fashion. With one full-time staff member and a part-time administrative support staff member, the program was drawing from numerous resources to offer an average of fifty learning opportunities every quarter by 2005. A trained team of staff members coordinated by a librarian offered basic, intermediate, and advanced sessions on the integrated library system. Members of the City/County Department of Human Resources provided managerial and supervisory courses as well as general courses on customer service basics and several other general interest topics. Staff from the City/County Department of Public Health provided health and safety sessions including disaster preparedness and two-hour ergonomic workshops designed for those who worked extensively with computer equipment and for those whose jobs required extensive lifting and bending. Dozens of instructors through the statewide Infopeople project provided day-long workshops designed to update information on reference tools, leadership skills, training techniques to be used for staff and members of the public, customer service, conflict resolution, and other subjects of interest to library staff. Infopeople is also developing online courses. Library training staff provided 60- and 90-minute introductions to Microsoft Office products, and staff were able to take specialized two-hour modules on Microsoft Office products through a local commercial training organization, Learn iT! Funding through the Friends of the Library extended learning opportunities by covering the cost of registration for staff interested in attending workshops offered regionally and nationally and also by partially supporting staff members' attendance at ALA, California Library Association, and other professional conferences. Key to the success of the program was the continuing support of several city librarians, library finance directors, and library human resources directors.

SHOWING THE VALUE OF TRAINING

A final area of leadership explored by the best workplace learning and performance professionals is continuing service as proponents of effective learning opportunities who show the positive impact such opportunities have both on the organization and on the clients it serves. Annual fights for budget dollars are common even in the best of times, and those who are able to show the results of workplace learning and development manage to retain organizational and financial support for training even in the most difficult of times.

There is widespread acknowledgment that documenting a return on the organization's investment of time and money increases the case to be made for continuation of training programs. Most of the trainer-teacher-learners we know, however, acknowledge that their efforts are generally limited to sharing anecdotes, being strong proponents for training within the organizations they serve, and documenting the favorable responses attendees provide at the conclusion of workplace learning and performance sessions. This a theme to which we return in chapter 7.

2

COLLABORATION
CREATING A COMMUNITY
OF LEARNING

Successful learning communities are all about finding and sustaining a sense of shared effort and interest.

—Char Booth, E-learning Librarian, University Library, University of California–Berkeley

When we are struggling to respond to a deluge of incoming phone calls, e-mail, text/instant messages, tweets, Facebook and LinkedIn updates, and people literally stopping us in hallways to ask for help, it can be difficult to remember that we, too, need learning resources and communities of support.

Many of us recognize that one of our greatest challenges is finding or making the time to continue our own professional development so that we can better serve those who learn from what we provide. We tend to fall into the same trap that our learners encounter: if we want to keep up with our daily workload *and* put out the fires blazing around us, we cut corners by not seeking the learning opportunities that are at the heart of our own continuing and long-term professional and personal development.

One extremely valuable resource for those committed to professional development is what have become known as communities of learning, communities of learners, or learning communities. The terms, like so many others we encounter and absorb in our era of instantaneous communication and viral marketing, have become ubiquitous. It is, therefore, easy to lose sight of people like Peter Senge, who through his book *The Fifth Discipline: The Art and Practice of the Learning Organization* has been instrumental in codifying a concept that is explored by others in ways ranging from face-to-face conversations to an article in Wikipedia.[1] It is not hard to see why the concept of communities of learning is so appealing. Whether we trace it to Senge or go back a few years earlier to sources cited in Wikipedia, we find it to be a concept that resonates deeply with trainer-teacher-learners, and for good reason: it feels like an archetypal model.

One popular example of a community of learning is the Learning 2.0, or 23 Things program, created by the Charlotte Mecklenburg Library.[2] In this program, members of library staff were encouraged to go through an online program where they learned twenty-three things that they needed to know about Web 2.0 technology. Each week's lesson came in the form of a podcast and blog post, and participants were required to create their own blogs to record their thoughts and experiences. The blogs from the participants were linked on the official 23 Things site, which enabled the participants to not only communicate and learn from each other but to also go through the experience of learning together. In a 2007 article, Helene Blowers, former technology director for the Charlotte Mecklenburg Library, recalls a branch manager saying, "How Learning 2.0 fostered teamwork and true fun I could write about for hours. Every time someone finished we all celebrated with them." Blowers continues:

> This thought, posted by a branch manager in her blog, embodies what is truly best about this new and different approach to learning—teamwork and community. Through the process of blogging itself staff members experienced an online community, but the added benefits of the program were the internal community building it provided both within branch locations and system-wide. Through the learning and knowledge exchanging process, self-proclaimed tech novices became experienced Learning 2.0 tutors to other staff members, and as confidences grew their learning discoveries branched out beyond 23 Things, creating avatars for themselves, playing with image generators, and constructing fun polls.[3]

Blowers is not alone in her efforts to inject fun and excitement into the learning process. "I think there is excitement in the different learning communities I am involved in at UCB," says Char Booth, e-learning librarian at the University Library, University of California, Berkeley.

> I have personally tried to up the interest ante of my colleagues in the area of emerging technology learning, which I have done in part by trying to make the tone of my trainings and marketing materials interesting, as well as by creating learning opportunities that sometimes have more of an "event" or "to-do" feel instead of the same old sessions

time and again. . . . Several of the topics that generated interest were then turned into longer-format technology trainings. . . . It was a great way to generate enthusiasm among a lot of potential learners—highly recommended. I like to moderate and emcee events like this, so I think I often end up being somewhat of a de facto organizational learning cheerleader, which is fine by me.

ARCHETYPAL COMMUNITIES OF LEARNING

As we look for recurring elements in successful communities of learning, we almost unintentionally fall into patterns that feel natural; then, if we are lucky, we stumble upon research confirming what we have found. Size, for example, does seem to matter. Members of one vibrant community—the ASTD Mt. Diablo chapter in the San Francisco East Bay area—had extensive discussions, during a strategic planning process, about what the ideal number of members for the group might be. Noting that one of the chapter's greatest strengths was having enough members to sustain the organization's activities while retaining a small enough group to support the sense of collegiality that attracted many to join, chapter board members eventually settled on a figure of 150—though noting that they would certainly not turn away the 151st person who wanted to join if the chapter grew to that level. Less than a few months later, one of us was finally reading Malcolm Gladwell's *The Tipping Point* and came across his summary of British anthropologist Robin Dunbar's rule of 150: "The figure of 150 seems to represent the maximum number of individuals with whom we can have a genuinely social relationship, the kind of relationship that goes with knowing who they are and how they relate to us."[4] As we applied that theory to what we were seeing in highly productive communities of learning—including the widely admired 23 Things program—we realized that even the largest learning organizations function well with smaller communities contributing to the larger organization's operations. Charlotte Mecklenburg Library initially had 352 participants, but many of those participants self-subdivided into smaller groups with coworkers from their library branches.

Moving one step further into an examination of archetypes that work in learning, we explored models of learning themselves. When we began with current formal training models including hour-long or half-day or full-day, one-time workshops and then broadened our thinking to include limited-duration series such as a one- or multipart weekly webinar series or online courses designed to fill workplace learning gaps, we eventually found ourselves contemplating more expansive formats. This ultimately led us to the model that is rare in workplace learning and performance programs but feels completely natural and productive to any of us who appreciated the seminal moments in our own educational process: courses that bring learners together for extended periods of time—a school or college quarter, semester, or multisemester period. The best of those experiences provided us—and continue to provide us—with ongoing sources of support from fellow students; instructors, professors, or guest lecturers; and advisors and other mentors who help us reach the potential we display and the learning goals we, our colleagues, and our managers and supervisors develop for us. That's what our communities of learning can give us outside formal academic settings, as our colleagues note.

Denver Public Library learning and development manager Sandra Smith, for example, jokingly says she started the Colorado Front Range Libraries Trainers Group ten years ago because she "was lonely one day." The serious result is that members continue to meet bimonthly "to share best practices, resources, support, [and] camaraderie" with a focus on "creating opportunities for library staff to be excellent at what they do." They vary meeting locations and, because of the composition of the group, are able to compare what is happening in public and academic libraries rather than remain within their individual work niches.

Another community of learning with national reach developed out of a biweekly live series of podcasts that are archived online as quickly as they can be recorded. Harford County Public Library technical trainer Maurice Coleman, a *Library Journal* 2010 "Mover and Shaker" and winner of the 2010 Citizens for Maryland Libraries Davis McCarn Award for "outstanding achievement that has improved library service and library advocacy in Maryland," started that successful online community through his biweekly *T is for Training* podcast series with a pilot program in August 2008. He taped his first official one-hour episode—"My Brain Is My Learning Environment"—the following month. Coleman's ability to create a community of learners for those involved in workplace learning and performance across the country met with instant success. Discussing serious topics while maintaining a sense of humor, several of the original participants continue to be involved in the program and are open to new participants. Coleman's ever-growing coalition of "usual suspects" often, during the live discussions, helps him identify the titles he tags onto the completed episodes before posting them in the show's archives.[5]

"The community came together as almost a happy accident and collection of people who have become friends [and] who happen to be in the same general line of work," Coleman says. He had met many of them through his visibility via social media such as Twitter and FriendFeed and through attendance at conferences. He also came to know them better through occasional meetings and phone conversations. "The show just tapped into that already existing network."

Coleman works with the support of his supervisor at the library and does everything he can to combine his efforts on the podcast with his efforts on behalf of his employer: "I use the show as a way to bring new and effective training ideas back to our system," he says, and he intentionally blurs the lines between his online and onsite work.

"The biggest difference between the *T is for Training* community and the Harford Public [Library] training community is that for *T is for Training* I just provide a space for the community to grow with a little direction, and with Harford County specific and specified organizational objectives usually provide direction for our training projects," he explains. "Those specific organizational objectives partnered with guided independent training make up our training atmosphere."

Coleman's advice to others attempting to create successful communities of learning: "Do your job well. Share your knowledge. Be an informal mentor. Be very visible in your organization for the right reasons. Stop and offer on-the-spot training whenever you can to whomever you can. Share your knowledge outside of your organization if opportunity arises. Attend local, regional, and national gatherings as often as you can. Share what you learn and how you learn with other people. Be nice to everyone."

Creating communities face-to-face and online are, Coleman suggests, similar endeavors. They are built upon a solid foundation of showing respect for others, responding promptly, being honest, and remembering to "share of yourself and your stories to better help others." Returning to the theme of our conversation, he concluded with the suggestion that we "encourage participation and leadership."

One interesting variation on the theme of communities of learning came out of an August 2010 *T is for Training* discussion. Participants were discussing a variety of related themes, including what Ray Oldenburg, in *The Great Good Place,* calls the third place.[6] In focusing on libraries' vital functions in their communities and the increasingly valuable services they provide as centers of learning for those needing to improve their job-searching skills and their ability to use the ever-changing technology that surrounds them, the idea for a fourth place was proposed: a community gathering place for social learning. It did not take long for those engaged in the conversation to agree that this was an idea well worth nurturing and promoting. Coleman, by the end of the hour-long online discussion, had provided the working definition just mentioned, and two blog posts were online a few days later.[7]

Participants, given the context of the conversation, were specifically thinking of libraries as this sort of fourth place. It is obvious, however, that there is room for fourth places of this level in almost any onsite or online setting where learners come and go, where they seek a community of support and a chance for Intersection-level exchanges—the *Intersection* being Frans Johansson's term, in *The Medici Effect,* for places where people of different backgrounds meet, exchange ideas, and develop and disseminate ideas they might otherwise not develop.[8] The Intersection, and the fourth place, themselves serve as and inspire communities of learning. It is also apparent that trainers as leaders are going to be the ones who make or break this idea of a fourth place in the months and years to come.

As we return to the larger theme of trainers as leaders within their organizations, we are particularly taken by Princeton Public Library assistant director Peter Bromberg's comments on the communities of learners he has joined and nurtured through his own professional endeavors: "You know, I was reading up on community of learners before our interview and I read this definition from Wikipedia:

> Community psychologists such as McMillan and Chavis (1986) state that there are four key factors that defined a sense of community: "(1) *membership,* (2) *influence,* (3) *fulfillment of individuals needs* and (4) *shared events and emotional connections.* So, the participants of learning community must feel some sense of loyalty and beyond to the group *(membership)* that drive their desire to keep working and helping others, also the things that the participant do . . . must affect what happened in the community, that means, an active and not just a reactive performance *(influence).* Besides a learning community must give the chance to the participants to meet particular needs *(fulfillment)* by expressing personal opinions, asking for help or specific information and share stories of events with particular issue included *(emotional connections)* emotional experiences.[9]

"And when I read that, I thought, 'That's our membership organization [the South Jersey Regional Library Cooperative, which closed after losing its funding in 2010]!'"

Bromberg also cites his "twittersphere" as one of the best communities of learning he has joined: "It might be stretching the formal definition of learning community, but I'm comfortable in letting the formal definition evolve to include my experience," he says. He also mentions the Library Garden blog group to which he contributed for four years (through July 2010), and he has been active for several years in the ALA Learning Round Table and its former incarnation, CLENERT.

"I think there's a certain amount of magic that either happens or doesn't," he notes in talking about the Library Garden blog group. "I think having an initial face-to-face meeting with the principles around a table, talking, sharing, and getting very excited was key. Also, Janie [Hermann], Robert [Lackie], Marie [Radford] and I all knew each other well and we enjoy each other immensely."

Char Booth, from the UC Berkeley Library, speaks with equal enthusiasm of the communities of learning she has joined: "The successful ones always seem to create diversity of opportunities—to offer different types of learning experiences as well as avenues for their members to create connections between one another and indicate their specializations. Successful learning communities are all about finding and sustaining a sense of shared effort and interest and also speaking usefully to an area of actual, practical need."

Among the things that become obvious as we look at successful communities of learning is that they are sustainable over a long period of time, are sometimes self-sustaining, and are far from static. Just as it is natural for employees to move from one organization to another as their careers progress, membership in dynamic communities of learning changes and evolves. Tracking the changes within two library-based communities of learning and a nonprofit community of learning later in this chapter helps us better understand how the process works.

FORMALLY AND INFORMALLY DEVELOPING COMMUNITIES OF LEARNING

At Denver Public Library, there is a deliberate attempt to create and support communities of learning and an overall community of learning, according to Sandra Smith. It is, she adds, part of what is expected of her, and she has a five-member training committee that supports her efforts. At the time of our interview, she had already been working for three years to implement the library's Employee Learning and Growth Program, which she calls "a major commitment by DPL to even more formalize our focus and strategic importance of a highly knowledgeable staff. . . . Every staff person is required, as part of their annual performance review, to do a certain number of learning opportunities and sharing activities. These can be from small to large, and the credit is earned by doing both—the sharing piece is as critical to my goal as is the actual individual learning."

Creating that program required "intensive communication" with the library's executive team and the twenty-five-member management team. "That was followed by more than twenty sessions to provide staff with information about the program, including forthright explanations of why the initiative was important to both the organization and to the individuals working here." A pilot project in spring 2009 involved forty-three members of library staff; the complete rollout took place approximately six months later.

Management consultant and trainer Pat Wagner echoes Smith's ideas about including management and adds that "people who love training and believe in the intrinsic value of training in the library often forget the purpose of training in the library: to focus on the better future of the people we serve. It's very easy to get caught up in the bells and whistles. Just because people go through training does not mean they learn anything."

"I think our community of learners benefits staff by providing them with convenient methods for accessing workplace learning and development," Jay Turner, training manager at Gwinnett County Public Library, says.

> My best example for this is how my organization provides a rich catalog of online learning content in our LMS [learning management system]. Staff members are free to explore the wealth of information therein, go through content at their convenience, and then apply any new or reinforced learning in their work unit. . . . I've heard anecdotally that some branches have staff members take the same online class at once so that the work unit as a whole can discuss content. That form of shared learning was used by a few branches when we deployed Microsoft Office 2007 for the entire organization.

Much that goes into developing and nurturing communities comes from the leaders within learning organizations, but, as Wagner notes, training needs to be part of the overall organization: "Training in a good organization should be work. It should be part of the expectation. [Otherwise] it's stuck on the wall with chewing gum. Everything else you do and now you have to fit in training."

A best practice from the business world is to incorporate time for learning into every employee's schedule on a weekly basis. This can be through formal or informal learning experiences, and we believe that if the time is not scheduled for every employee it is unlikely that the employee will be able to find the time to participate.

Wagner also points out that an organization becomes a learning organization when "we have emotionally healthy people; when people are treated well; when people have the tools they need to do their jobs. It is rare to have an unhealthy organization and turn that into a learning organization."

The bottom line is that training cannot be expected magically to fix serious problems within an organization. For example, offering conflict resolution training when the problem is caused by one person or offering stress management training to employees who have an abusive supervisor are not solutions that resolve problems effectively. These challenges require organizational changes or disciplinary action—not training. It takes a strong trainer-leader to avoid becoming a training "order taker" who serves up exactly what is requested. This is why many in the training industry have steered away from the term *training* and, instead, prefer *workplace learning and performance*. We are more than "just trainers." We are key people who help an organization and individuals succeed, reach their potential, and achieve their visions.

RECOGNIZING A LEARNING ORGANIZATION

"The main way that people at the top are going to create a learning organization is how people see them as learners," Pat Wagner suggests.

> My main evidence of it [an organization] as a learning organization is if the director shows up for training. If I walk into a room and there's the director and there's the head of HR and there's the branch managers and there's the administration—no matter how big or small the library is—I know that's a learning organization. If learning is for the rank and file then I know it is not a learning organization. There's a phoniness to it. Because the implication is when you get smart enough and rich enough and high enough in the food chain, one of your privileges is that you are now exempt from having to learn. I love it when I walk into a workshop and there's the director and I walk up and say, "What are you doing here? You could teach this class," and they say, "I always learn something new and I have to send the right message to staff that learning is what smart people do."

Peter Bromberg echoes this idea that learning starts through the example set by leaders:

> Well, you know the old saying: a fish rots from the head down. I think that's true for most elements of organizational culture. It starts at the top. If the head or heads of the organization are curious people, who want to know why things work, and how things work, then a culture of learning will flow from that. If the heads of the organization are either too busy or not wired to think curiously, then it becomes difficult to have an organizationally based community of learners.

"I do think a community of learners almost has to be self-sustaining," he adds. "I don't think you can force people to be in a community of learners. . . . I think communities of learners self-organize to a large extent—especially in social networking spaces."

"The whole focus on being a learning organization . . . is critical to the long-term strategic relevance of the library to the community," Sandra Smith says of the Denver Public Library.

> If our staff are not able to show good results for the individuals and stakeholders in the community—through their knowledge and skills—then the library itself will be seen as marginal and at-risk. This is happening now, and it is critical for a learning organization to ensure that their staff understand this and what their role is in making the outcome positive. Tying this all into a library's fundamental operating principles and strategy is vital for it happening within the organization.

"I think excitement about learning *is* our organization," Bromberg said of the South Jersey Regional Library Cooperative while he was serving as assistant director for that organization:

> It runs through everything we do seamlessly. [Learning is] definitely not seen as an obligation. We are curious people! And learning/doing new things is what's fun for us. (The hard part is tending to the garden once it's planted, and not rushing off to plant a new one.) Again, being that we're a small organization . . . we support it. It goes back to the fact that we are all curious—our office manager is curious! We all enjoy learning, talking, sharing. That's the organization that Karen Hyman [former executive director for the cooperative] consciously built.

It does not take large numbers of people to initiate communities of learning, Janet Hildebrand, deputy county librarian for the Contra Costa County Library system, suggests:

> I believe that by starting with willing volunteers, however few, and putting your energy into supporting them to lead and spread their excitement and demonstrate what can be done, you gradually have more and more people who see that they want to step forward and be involved too, and that eventually reaches a critical mass where they are in the majority. In that sense, it becomes more and more perpetuating and self-sustaining in that there is momentum in the direction of trying new things and learning and focusing forward into the future.

However, there is always a need for leadership. . . . Good training and implementation experiences have to be planned in such a way that they work, or the participants do not have the clear experience of contribution and progress that makes the next one go easily. Many of the participants can become leaders, but there will always need to be leaders, organizers, visionaries for each area of learning.

Jay Turner reminds us that sustainability among communities of learning comes from the natural appeal of those groups:

My overarching philosophy for supporting workplace learning is to create an atmosphere where learning is fun and where people are empowered to learn on their own terms. I do this by making sure that there are relevant professional development opportunities available, ensuring that we have training to support the organization's objectives and that everyone can play at some point during learning. I also believe in making myself available formally and informally to all staff members to support them in their growth.

"If we can create excitement, I think to some extent we can create a community of learners," Catherine Vaughn, continuing education coordinator for the Lee County Library System, maintains.

But that is only half the battle—the participants must be willing to participate and learn and then, most importantly, go back and apply the new knowledge, share the new knowledge with colleagues, and continue to build upon the new knowledge and skills. Learning, as you know, is a fifty-fifty game. It must be a sharing process on both sides—instructor and participant—in order to be successful. Also, the supervisor plays a big role in getting the participant ready for the session and then to keep the enthusiasm going, and that is where I feel we falter. Supervisors don't realize the dramatic role they play in educating their staff.

Louise Whitaker, training coordinator for Oklahoma's Pioneer Library System, was among those who were intentionally working to create and foster a community of learners as we were writing this book. She explains:

This year, we are starting to be a lot more intentional about providing different ways for our staff to have learning opportunities, rather than just the traditional face-to-face meetings. We are using WebEx for synchronous trainings. We did a few last year, I did one Tuesday, and we have two each month (minimum). The other advantage to using WebEx is that it is recorded, so if someone can't attend the WebEx session, and they can't attend the face-to-face session, they can at least listen to and review the recording so they are not hearing only what the facilitator is saying but what other staff are saying—the input on the topic.

There was also a big focus on an individual's responsibility in online training. In an online training, there is going to be more independent work that is required, whether it's reading articles and discussing that with other staff or finding articles on their own. It's moving away from just having someone stand in front and talking to them, and it's a different model than what we're used to in a traditional classroom setting. They've been very enthusiastic. I think it's going to change [the way people interact in and support a community of learning] because one of the things we're going to develop—if five people have taken the same online training, they as a group will get together and discuss the content of the training and also articles pertinent to that topic.

There are, Whitaker notes, a variety of actions she and her colleagues can take to make that community of learners self-sustaining:

We've been working with a consultant on our pay compensation. We were talking yesterday about core competencies—developing those. . . . One of the things that came out of the staff group was that learning should be one of our core competencies. This was just the first meeting, the first discussion, on core competencies. . . . The consultant will give us the result from the two meetings. We'll look at it as an administrative group and filter it back down to staff to develop six or seven core competencies for all staff. I was excited that learning was one of the competencies that staff felt was important. We were working from a list of fifty or sixty suggestions.

The Charlotte Mecklenburg Library is creating a similar model of learning communities with its e-learning program implemented in 2010. The library's intranet, created with Drupal, hosts learning forums or online discussion boards. Staff who attend training—whether face-to-face, online synchronously, or asynchronously—are required to post reflections after their training. The discussion boards are moderated by learning facilitators who encourage staff to learn beyond the confines of the classroom, whether it be physical or virtual. This is also a place to address the many questions that arise during training but get "parked" because the questions are unrelated to the training or there is not enough time to answer them all.

ALA LEARNING ROUND TABLE

As we examined model communities of learning featuring trainers as leaders, we were quickly and naturally drawn to ALA's Learning Round Table because it offers a pattern discernable elsewhere and because we are much involved with the group. The group's blog, *ALA Learning*, has a clear mission statement: to serve as a "source for training and learning news, information, best practices, and thoughtful discussion."[10] Its leaders and supporting members come and go depending on workplace and personal commitments and challenges. Even the name of the group has changed, but there is a consistency of purpose and support that provides long-term stability.

Many of us who are currently involved in the Round Table—including several of the people interviewed for this book—were drawn to the organization through colleagues' recommendations and an obvious attraction to it as the potential fourth place—that community gathering place for social learning—mentioned earlier in this chapter.

Records posted online by Round Table member Anne Masters, director at Pioneer Library System in Oklahoma, trace the group's origins to the mid-1970s, when it was formed as the Continuing Library Education and Networking Exchange Round Table (CLENERT).[11] It became an ALA round table in 1983 and continued to flourish under a series of presidents including Gail McGovern, who later became deeply involved in the California-based Infopeople project; Duncan Smith, a founding partner of NoveList, a wonderful database that helps match readers with books of interest to them; Pat Carterette, who succombed to cancer in January 2011; and Sharon Morris, Jasmine Posey, Cheryl Rogers, and Stacy Schrank, who remain active in state and local libraries across the country and in the Learning Round Table.

As the group continues to grow adept at using online resources to keep members connected between ALA's two annual gatherings, Learning Round Table members increasingly contact each other through monthly online meetings, a blog featuring contributions from a stable of writers involved in workplace learning in libraries and other organizations throughout the United States, a newsletter disseminated to Round Table members and posted online, and workshops and other activities offered face-to-face at ALA conferences and online with collaborators, including the WebJunction library learning community.

Jay Turner, among those who mention the ALA Learning Round Table as one of their most valued communities of learners, explains: "We're a group with diverse interests, backgrounds, and skills always looking to share knowledge. I like how we're able to engage and share, even when we aren't doing so for official work of the Round Table."

"It gives me an opportunity to interact with people that I'm not going to meet otherwise," Louise Whitaker agreed in a separate interview. "Jay Turner is a perfect example. When I grow up, I want to be just like Jay." She went on to add: "Everybody has a little different take on training and how they do it at their organization. That interaction, among the group, the ideas that flow—where else am I going to get those ideas if I'm just sitting at my desk? I'm not going to grow as a learner."

In summary, the Learning Round Table—for those of us involved—is a group with a rich and treasured tradition of service and innovation, one that draws us together when are looking for human-scale contact among twenty thousand or more colleagues attending national conferences, and as a place to turn for first-rate counsel and creative solutions when we struggle with our own workplace learning and performance challenges. It is where we meet colleagues who become friends and collaborators on projects we might not otherwise consider—including this book—and an organization that continually reminds us how important it is to combine our onsite and online relationships in ways that benefit us and all whom we serve.

PACIFIC LIBRARY PARTNERSHIP STAFF DEVELOPMENT COMMITTEE

Although the Pacific Library Partnership Staff Development Committee meets only once every two months, members engage in lively exchanges the likes of which we find nowhere else, produce an annual conference and at least one other event for staff of libraries throughout our service area, and work to disseminate ideas and innovations among members and the staff of the libraries relying on us for learning opportunities they otherwise would not have.

Like the Learning Round Table, the group has a clear mandate: fill unmet training needs for library staff members within its service area. It has also had more names over the course of its existence than any of us can remember. When one of us writing this book joined the committee several years ago, the group was the training branch of a San Francisco Bay area library consortium, the Golden Gateway Library Network (GGLN). The Network eventually went out of business, but the committee did not disband. Committee members who valued the collaborations and what those collaborations produced obtained permission from the directors of the libraries they served to continue meeting as part of their regular staff duties. Relying on the Peninsula Library System (a consortium of thirty-two city, county, and community college libraries in San Mateo County) as its fiscal agent, the committee eventually adopted the name "The Library Staff Development Committee of the Greater Bay Area." Events for members of library support staff each spring and an annual Future of Libraries conference each September (the sixth annual conference was held in September 2010) continued to draw attention to the group. When committee members were offered the chance to become part of the newly formed Pacific Library Partnership in 2009, the committee's name again changed—this time to the Pacific Library Partnership Staff Development Committee.

What makes the committee worth examining is the way its members seamlessly and effectively work together; the planning and implementation process for the annual Future of Libraries conference presents a model that can easily be adapted by others. Although there is an ebb and flow to membership, with some members having joined as recently as 2010 and others having been active for a decade or more, it does not take long for individuals to find a way to apply their own skills and interests to the benefit of the entire group. A long-term member who is superb at marketing committee events routinely assumes that role and accomplishes it in ways that often leave no empty seats in the session venues. One or two committee members generally, without any overt arm twisting, step up to the role of event chair or cochair each year. There is a fine balance of continuity and innovation from year to year, so basic systems do not have to be re-created, but event formats and content evolve to keep presentations interesting for repeat attendees.

Every step of the planning process is completely collaborative—to the point that it is often difficult to connect a specific idea to an individual committee member. There is little attention paid to a contributor's title or position on the committee; effective committee chairs or cochairs facilitate meetings in such a way that everyone contributes to conversations about the events during bimonthly meetings, and those responsible for implementing individual aspects such as marketing, or contacting prospective speakers, or making lunch arrangements for presenters and committee members, or serving as liaisons with representatives of the libraries where events are being held complete their tasks between meetings. The result is that as much work is done between meetings as during meetings; each meeting becomes a productive and collegial combination of providing updates, planning next steps, and doing whatever is necessary to produce events that are appealing and rewarding to attendees; and members of this well-functioning community of learners look forward to rather than dread meetings—quite an achievement at a time when so many of us only half-jokingly say we would rather kill ourselves than join another organization requiring attendance at meetings.

ASTD MT. DIABLO CHAPTER

ASTD is probably one of the best nonprofit organizations and communities of learners where trainers as leaders can hone and display their skills. It is disappointing, therefore, to find no more than a handful of library trainers actively involved in their local chapters or national ASTD committees and conferences. Involvement in ASTD works both ways: those involved in library workplace learning and performance programs have much to learn from nonprofit and corporate programs, and those involved in nonprofit and corporate programs could gain much from their library colleagues. The active ASTD chapter members we have found among our library colleagues tend to be the same people we see as active participants in the ALA Learning Round Table; others seem to have a peripheral connection to ASTD through memberships purchased by their organizations but have or make little time to attend ASTD functions, read ASTD publications, or take advantage of ASTD online resources.

The forty thousand trainer-teacher-learners spread among more than 130 chapters in the United States and more than thirty international partners include those who volunteer as board members, serve on national committees, and volunteer to run programs that serve members and guests. Many trainers who assume chapter board responsibilities face the same challenges newcomers to library training programs face: they are new to leadership in general and management specifically, so they learn at the same time that they are carrying out their responsibilities. They have to learn quickly and often find that changing circumstances in their professional and personal lives can force them to move to other endeavors just when they are becoming comfortable in the workplace learning and performance roles they have assumed. ASTD chapter board members' terms of office are generally one year long—a period that passes quickly for those who have to learn while they are serving; some chapters create two-year terms and stagger elections so that no more than half of all board members are up for reelection or replacement at a time—a system that creates more continuity at the board level and provides more opportunities for leaders to use what they have learned.

Board member orientation and training vary widely from chapter to chapter, just as leadership and management training for library and nonprofit organization trainers varies. Staff and volunteers from the national organization provide numerous online and face-to-face resources for current and prospective chapter leaders. The parent organization hosts an annual chapter leader conference to help board-level volunteers gain the leadership and management skills they need while meeting colleagues from across the country, but fewer than half of all board members are able to attend that two-day annual learning opportunity. Rapid turnover at the chapter board level, furthermore, can result in tremendous variations in the quality of leadership and the direction followed by chapter leaders from year to year.

One of the greatest dangers arising out of this inconsistency is that a chapter that is managed well one year can quickly take a severe downturn the following year, and those with just a few years of inadequate leadership and poor engagement at the general membership level can quickly go out of business. The obvious parallel between what happens with ASTD chapters and what happens in library and nonprofit workplace learning and performance programs is on display when a training director leaves and is replaced by someone far less effective.

A positive example of a community of learners nearly fading away and then making a strong comeback is the Mt. Diablo chapter, which operates directly north of Silicon Valley, in two densely populated counties—Contra Costa and Alameda—and draws members from an area that overlaps other nearby chapters. Mt. Diablo elected its first board president in 1988. The organization, like many other chapters, has undergone strong periods of growth and equally strong periods of decline. As members come and go, parts of the chapter's history have been lost—which forces those who remain to struggle with rebuilding without the benefit of their predecessors' experiences. The chapter's most recent decline, in the middle of 2007, saw overall membership shrink to nearly sixty members—compared to estimates ranging from one hundred and fifty to two hundred members at the chapter's peak. When a longtime member stepped back in to try to save the chapter from extinction, there were fewer than ten board members in place, business often had to be delayed because a quorum was not present to take official actions, and several board members were caught up asking a question commonly asked by members of weaker ASTD chapters: what value does the national organization offer to local chapters—an odd question when one considers that without that national organization the local chapters would not even have a name under which to operate.

Rebuilding the chapter took nearly three years, and the process is not yet complete as this summary is being written. The three most active members of the nine-member board met throughout 2008 to rewrite the chapter's bylaws in accordance with a model provided by the parent organization, then gained the support of other board members to adopt the updated document. Clearly defining the way the chapter would operate at the local level in collaboration with regional chapters and the parent organization, the updated bylaws laid the foundations for a chapter that was in partnership with, rather than opposed to, the very organization that chartered it. Furthermore, the new bylaws defined the way chapter leaders are recruited—through a nominating committee comprising board and non-board members so that the board would not become too distanced from the general membership it served. A third critically important element helped pave the way for a potentially healthy nonprofit organization of trainers serving as leaders of other trainers: all board positions were defined in ways that called for individuals to work with rather than against other board colleagues in fulfilling the specific duties of their own positions.

The next step in rebuilding the organization—which was seeing a slow and steady increase in membership throughout 2008 because of improvements in monthly programs and a responsiveness to what members said they wanted to learn from the keynote speakers who appeared at the chapter's monthly dinner meetings—came in the form of rewritten job descriptions. Fleshing out the broad position descriptions contained within the bylaws, the board president and president-elect worked with individual board members to craft descriptions reflecting current and proposed roles and responsibilities. The focus remained on attracting board members who would work collaboratively to implement newly adopted mission, vision, and value statements consistent with the parent organization's mission and core values. The payoff came in the second half of 2009, when a fully engaged board approved the new board job descriptions and moved into the final phase of a year-long effort to create a three-year strategic plan drafted by board and non-board members of the chapter.

When that strategic plan was finally adopted by a combination of new and returning board members in early 2010, the final foundational step to be completed was creation of a strong marketing and communications plan designed to serve members and reach prospective members to assure the chapter's long-term growth and sustainability. The process and results were stronger than anyone would have imagined when they began. A marketing and communications task force that began as a subset of the entire board eventually included participation from nearly every active board member; grew to include a couple of non-board chapter members; attracted a former board president who had not been active in chapter activities during the previous five years; and even included a marketing and communications expert whose brief interactions with the chapter drew him into the process even though he lives more than 300 miles from the chapter's home base.

MOVING OUTSIDE OUR WALLS

What everything in this chapter suggests to trainers—whether they are working in libraries, nonprofit organizations, or for-profit businesses—is that there is a lot to be gained by moving outside the walls of their own organizations in ways that provide them with professional development opportunities and interactions with workplace learning and performance colleagues who are working in settings much different from their own. What all of us learn from these leadership opportunities prepares us to better participate as leaders in the organizations we serve—whether we are full-time employees, part-time employees, contract workers, or consultants. The ultimate beneficiaries are the learners we assist, the organizations that rely on us to create what ASTD refers to as "a world that works better," and the customers who benefit from what our organizations provide.

NOTES

1. Peter Senge, *The Fifth Discipline: The Art and Practice of the Learning Organization,* 2nd ed. (New York: Currency Doubleday, 2006); "Learning Community," Wikipedia, http://en.wikipedia.org/wiki/Learning_communities.
2. Charlotte Mecklenburg Public Library, "Learning 2.0," http://plcmcl2-about.blogspot.com.
3. Helene Blowers and Lori Reed, "The C's of Our Sea Change: Plans for Training Staff, from Core Competencies to LEARNING 2.0," *Computers in Libraries,* February 2007: 14–15.
4. Malcolm Gladwell, *The Tipping Point: How Little Things Can Make a Big Difference* (New York: Little, Brown, 2000), 179. A serviceable introduction to Dunbar's rule of 150 is also available at "Dunbar's Number," http://en.wikipedia.org/wiki/Dunbar%27s_number.
5. *T is for Training,* http://tisfortraining.wordpress.com. Episode 40, "I Reject Your Reality," and episode 44, "I Am in a Library of Three People and the Other Two Are Bitter," are two good samples of the spirit of what the group produces.
6. "T is for Training 53: Creating the 4th Place: A Community Gathering Place for (Social) Learning," http://tisfortraining.wordpress.com/2010/08/13/t-is-for-training-53-creating-the-4th-place-a-community-gathering-place-for-social-learning. Oldenburg suggests that our first place is our home, our second place is where we work, and our third place is the treasured community meeting place where we, our friends, and our colleagues come and go; see Ray Oldenburg, *The Great Good Place: Cafés, Coffee Shops, Bookstores, Bars, Hair Salons and Other Hangouts at the Heart of a Community* (New York: Marlowe, 1989).
7. Paul Signorelli, "Community, Collaboration, and Learning: Time for the Fourth Place," *Building Creative Bridges,* August 15, 2010, http://buildingcreative bridges.wordpress.com/2010/08/15/community-collaboration-and-learning-time-for-the-fourth-place; and

Jill Hurst-Wahl, "Community, Collaboration, and Learning: Time for the Fourth Place," *Digitization 101*, August 17, 2010, http://hurstassociates.blogspot.com.

8. Frans Johansson, *The Medici Effect: Breakthrough Insights at the Intersection of Ideas, Concepts, and Cultures* (Boston: Harvard Business School Press, 2004).

9. Wikipedia, "Learning Community," http://en.wikipedia.org/wiki/Learning_communities.

10. ALA Learning Round Table, "About ALA Learning," http://alalearning.org/about/about-ala-learning/.

11. Ann Masters, "CLENE History," December 2006, http://alalearning.org/documents/clene_history_dec_06.pdf.

3

TRAINERS AS INTERNAL CONSULTANTS AND FACILITATORS OF CHANGE

Being an internal consultant means that . . . I have a high
degree of autonomy over how the training function operates.

—Jay Turner, Training Manager, Gwinnett County Public Library

The idea of trainers serving as consultants within their own organizations is relatively new to libraries and nonprofit organizations. It requires a delicate balance, often filled with unwritten rules governing organizational politics and how to juggle our roles as employees and as agents of change. Trainers-as-leaders within many libraries and nonprofit organizations have admitted that their own staff give more credibility to outside consultants than to an internal employee functioning as a consultant.

No topic revealed more uncertainty as well as discomfort during our interviews than that of trainers-as-leaders playing the role of internal consultants as they help facilitate positive, sustainable change. This actually is not much of a surprise since so many workplace learning and performance practitioners who work full-time within a single organization are, by the nature of their jobs, forced to deal with an overwhelming number of responsibilities. There is little encouragement or time provided for the level of personal development and research at the heart of the consulting process. Politics is also important in consulting on any level, but an outside consultant has the ability to pack up and leave at the end of the job, whereas an internal consultant may be around for years dealing with the consequences of what was done or what he or she tried to do to improve the organization.

If we are going to be effective leaders within our organizations, we are going to have to alter this situation, for it is only through the act of stepping back from short-term duties and challenges, continually scanning the environments in which we and our learners function, and coming back with a comprehensive view of what our organizations need that we will be in a position to create, nurture, and sustain the communities of learning that are essential to success for us, for our learners, and for the organizations and customers and clients we ultimately must serve.

Both of us, in our relationships with short-term clients and long-term employers, have experienced critically important moments of revelation that help us understand when something is terribly wrong and must be resolved. These are lessons not easily learned and absorbed; we, like our colleagues, have had to struggle with the repercussions of such moments.

Let's be explicit: as leaders in workplace learning and performance improvement, we must determine when training is needed or when another solution is appropriate. Many organizations, rather than deal with poor processes, counter-intuitive software, or ineffective leadership, make the mistake of offering training as a solution rather than seeking ways to resolve problems with more appropriate and effective solutions. If we function as trainers/order takers and provide training upon request without any analysis or investigation, we run the risk of standing in front of a class of peers and avoiding any acknowledgment of the elephant in the room that we are all judiciously attempting to ignore. When training is needed, we must take the time to analyze the situation as an outside consultant would and investigate any hidden causes that led to the need for training.

When we find ourselves working beyond our physical, mental, and emotional capabilities and realize that our efforts are not producing the necessary results, we also need to remember that thinking and acting and serving as consultants are aspects of what we always should be doing. We need to use all that we know to identify the overall issues, look for solutions beyond those that are not currently working, and bring those potential solutions to the attention of anyone capable of advocating and implementing more effective ideas and processes.

We cannot be too direct in addressing the dangers inherent in this situation; the risks of suggesting and advocating change can be enormous. If we are too far outside what our organizations are willing to consider, we run the risk of isolating ourselves rather than remaining engaged in the process of change. If, on the other hand, we take no action because we fear losing whatever influence we have managed to develop, we run an even greater risk—that of becoming cynical and dispirited. This, of course, leads to burnout. It also removes any possibility that we can be the leaders needed in workplace learning and performance.

As we read the best books and articles we can find on consulting and talk with other consultants who produce positive results, we are struck by a basic realization that is far from new or revolutionary: effective consulting and training are seamlessly intertwined. Both are grounded in a need for some sort of change, and both produce change through a process of facilitating the development of cohesive communities akin to what we discussed in the previous chapter, on communities of learning.

It is somewhat frustrating, therefore, to find that few of us involved in the day-to-day planning, development, implementation, evaluation, and revision of workplace learning and performance programs think of ourselves as *consultants* within our own organizations—internal consultants rather than external consultants brought into organizations for a limited period to complete a well-defined, finite project. Because we do not often have enough—or perhaps do not insist on having—the time to hone our skills as internal consultants, we inadvertently contribute to a situation in which our administrators, managers and supervisors, and staff colleagues give more credibility to an outside trainer than to their on-staff colleagues. An irony in this situation is that some trainers-as-leaders appear to garner more attention and praise outside the organizations that employ them than they do from their own administrators—although we must quickly add that many learners do acknowledge and express abundant amounts of gratitude for the effects in-house trainers have when they take on a consultant's frame of mind and serve as advocates of first-rate learning opportunities.

BRINGING VALUE

A great beginning point for us as we initially consider the important and effective roles we can play as consultants within our organizations is a brief exploration of what the best consultants actually do. Writer-consultant Alan Weiss suggests at the beginning of his book *Million Dollar Consulting* that a consultant "is someone who provides value through specialized expertise, content, behavior, skill, or other resources to assist a client in improving the status quo in return for mutually agreed compensation"—certainly a description that often fits those involved in effective workplace learning and performance programs. Furthermore, Weiss continues, consulting "is not synonymous with implementing, delivering, instructing, or executing, although consulting may include any of these activities"—a reminder that many of us must be adept at recognizing and moving between those varied roles. He also provides samples of consulting goals expressed by his colleagues that help us see we are not as far removed from the consulting role as we might initially have assumed: designing and implementing workshops that produce quantifiable change; entering into collaborative relationships; and "enhancing the productivity of their people through needs analyses, enhanced communication, and joint decision making."[1]

Peter Block, in *Flawless Consulting*, is even more eloquent: "The core transaction of any consulting contract is the transfer of expertise from the consultant to the client"—something we believe is inherent in the best of our day-to-day work as trainers-as-leaders. "Most people in staff roles in organizations are really consultants, even if they don't officially call themselves 'consultants,'" Block maintains. "Staff people function in any organization by planning, recommending, assisting or advising." The difference between consulting and managing, he notes, is the difference between guiding actions and taking action: "The moment you take direct responsibility, you are acting as a manager"—which, of course, provides more support for internal consultants who must be able to move facilely from role to role while remaining cognizant of the benefits and risks that accompany those shifts.[2]

Block's work has had a tremendous influence on many of us, and one of our colleagues, Denver Public Library learning and development manager Sandra Smith, refers to *Flawless Consulting* as a "must-live-by [book] for all trainers." "I was so proud of reading that book a while back and finding out that I was doing so much of what he recommended, and I didn't know why, other than it worked!" Smith added.

Block, like Weiss, sees clear connections between consulting and training-teaching-learning: "While we usually claim that we are in the business of helping our clients learn, most traditional educational or consulting efforts are more about teaching than learning. If you ask who is really learning at any meeting, communication session, or training event, the answer is usually the person in charge. . . . To bring value to the participant or the client, we need to design our efforts to support learning at the expense of teaching."[3]

Toward the end of *Flawless Consulting*, Block turns back to a theme we explore at greater length in chapter 4: the detrimental impact of stress and competition on learning. He suggests that as consultants we "are responsible for one another's learning" and need to do all we can to foster collaboration rather than competition in the learning opportunities we provide.[4] Those interested in spending more time with Block and reading his thoughts on internal consulting will find plenty of rewards throughout his book, but particularly in chapter 7.

A substantial and significant role of trainers as leaders is to help learners learn how to learn, and there is no area where the role of trainers as consultants within their own organizations is as clear and essential, as we gather while reading

Gordon and Ronald Lippitt's *The Consulting Process in Action:* "We believe that systematic planning of any necessary learning session is an ethical responsibility of every professional helper," they insist. "Developing a good design for participative learning facilitates the client's readiness and flexibility with regard to changing plans when new needs emerge"[5]—familiar material for trainers who use the ADDIE (analysis, design, development, implementation, and evaluation) model or its slightly updated sibling, ARDDIE (which adds a formal research phase into the process).[6]

The Lippitt brothers, like Block, strongly acknowledge the connection between consulting and training/educating:

> Consulting about innovations may require training and education within the client system. The consultant may be a creator of learning experiences or a direct teacher, using the skills of a designer, leader, and evaluator of the learning process.... We believe that every internal and external consultant should be able to function in this role. The capacity to train and educate is essential to many helping situations, particularly when a specific learning process is indicated in order for the client system to acquire competence in certain areas.[7]

They also discuss consultants' functions as "objective observers" and remind us that part of "the function of the objective observer is to ask questions that help the client to clarify and confront the problem involved and to make decisions. The consultant may also paraphrase, probe, and be empathic, experiencing with the client the blocks that initially provoked the problem. In this role the consultant acts as a philosopher taking a long-range view"[8]—again, a reminder that as leaders we need to be helping to define what problems training is designed to address as much as we need to be involved in delivering solutions through learning opportunities.

The Lippitt brothers do not shy away from the potential challenges we face as internal consultants:

> The consultant who is subordinate to the same supervisor as the group that he or she is working with frequently is forced into the role of police officer or watchdog. . . . Role expectations for internal consultants are limited insofar as they are not independent agents and their functions within organizations are specified. In addition to encountering resentment for intervening, the internal consultant must face preconceived notions of how much he or she will tell the supervisor and what specific changes will be effected.[9]

Block echoes this challenge as well—"As an internal consultant, you are at every moment embedded in some part of the hierarchy and the current politics of the organization"—and goes on to say that the internal consultant has his or her own manager to please and his or her own department's goals to support.[10] Consulting with colleagues in another department can bring conflict where none existed. It is also, on the other hand, an opportunity to step beyond the role of being "just a trainer" and function as one who can bring change and performance improvement to the organization.

The Lippitts' commitment to the connection between consulting and training-teaching-learning is so complete that they devote an entire chapter to the basics of designing effective learning opportunities—a wonderful resource for anyone new to workplace learning and performance. Their list of resources at the end of their chapter on consultants' roles is also highly recommended for anyone interested in more information on the topic.

If we want to serve as learning consultants helping others learn how to learn more effectively, we can also draw from resources including Andrew Jefferson, Roy Pollock, and Calhoun Wick's creatively designed *Getting Your Money's Worth from Training and Development*—inventive not only because it is a straightforward, easy-to-digest guide offering learning tips to managers and employees but because it is printed in flipbook fashion, with one half of the book directed to the managers and the other, when readers flip the book over, directed to the participants.[11] This gives all readers the advantage of seeing the ways managers' and employees' roles in the learning process differ and the ways they overlap and is in itself a learning experience in that it helps cultivate potential leaders while they are in subordinate positions within their organizations.

There is even more to consider as we consultants help others learn to learn. As increasing amounts of learning within libraries, nonprofits, and other organizations move to online environments, we need to be facilitating the dual challenge of learning the subject matter being offered while also learning how to master that subject matter in a distance-learning environment. We can overcome this challenge by sharing and using resources available to us, rather than hoarding those resources, to better understand all that the transition implies for us and for our learners.[12]

The good news is that online learning is far from new; segments of our audience have had distance-learning experiences via radio, television, or correspondence courses. What is different now is the use of contemporary digital tools including comprehensive online learning management systems such as Blackboard and Angel; online conferencing tools with audio or video capabilities such as WebEx, Dimdim, GoToMeeting, TalkShoe, and others that seem to spring up faster than we can keep track of them[13]; and even social networking tools such as Skype, Google Chat/Talk, Facebook, and LinkedIn discussion groups become places for online student-trainer interactions.[14]

As we consider all these various and varied interweavings of workplace learning and performance and what we might do as consultants within our own organizations, we receive confirmation from at least a couple of our colleagues that our leadership in this area is critically important: "Anyone responsible for training must consider the organization they work in—how it works, who makes it work," Denver Public's Smith reminds us.

> People make things happen and trainers must utilize (or create) their ability to work with individuals and systems. Trainers must see themselves as problem-solvers for the big and small picture, and likewise as personal problem-solvers for every manager—our job is to help them make their jobs successful. . . . Impactful communication around this is critical and trainers must take the initiative to show that they are solutions and key contributors—and offer the how and whys and any other evidence they can to become at least relevant, if not essential, to the work that goes on throughout the library.

One major change initiative ("Beyond Today") that Smith helped facilitate in Denver involved changes in the job duties of senior librarians in her organization: "I was brought into the conversation initially on 'how do we make this happen without them blowing their tops?' After we figured out the big picture communication, I was 'consulted' as to how to determine what the new skills needed to be. Rough ideas were out there but needed to be refined."

Smith determined ways to communicate the need for acquisition of the new skills and then developed the training program that all senior librarians were required to attend. "The program . . . was a series of sessions focused on everything from supervising to new technologies, to building management. I was a key person [in producing] the final result of our senior librarians operating successfully in a new role in the organization."

CHANGE IS FINE—AS LONG AS IT'S FOR YOU, NOT ME

At the heart of this chapter is the idea that trainers as internal consultants are facilitators of change—a process that does not come easily to most of us and certainly is not easily completed within libraries and nonprofit organizations.

Karen Hyman, former executive director for the South Jersey Regional Library Cooperative, facetiously and memorably captured a truism she called "The Rule of 1965" for libraries (and, we would suggest, many other organizations with well-established traditions) in an article she wrote for *American Libraries* magazine in 1999: anything done before a certain point in time (in this case, before 1965) is seen as basic; "everything else is extra," she writes. "For decades libraries have dealt with change by setting limits that marginalize what we do and ensure that library services are sometimes good but rarely essential to any but the neediest or the most determined. Often the limits hang around forever, well beyond growing pains or economic imperative, defended vociferously by those born after the original change took place."[15]

This, Contra Costa County Library deputy county librarian Janet Hildebrand says, is where trainers as consultants are critical:

> The trainer-consultant should passionately believe in the power of learning—that to most human beings, even those who seem jaded, worn out, set in their ways, there is something life-affirming and contagious about learning and being successful at something you couldn't imagine being about to do. So, especially when looking at a whole group or staff of a library, one should never assume that they won't change, or they can't possibly become what our library has become. When managed well from the top, when building from the small beginnings and focusing energy on building it, this [change] will come about because, fundamentally, most people like to feel good about themselves, and learning is the path to that.

There is no denying that we have to recognize and laugh at our own foibles and limitations if we are going to be effective in facilitating change in others. It is a great reminder, as we participate in meetings where we are planning changes for others, or when we are at the front of a classroom or in the facilitator's seat during a live online webinar, that there are certain things we, ourselves, do not want to alter. Suggest, for example, that we switch from a coffeehouse or restaurant that we adore to something new and therefore unfamiliar, and we immediately recognize that it is not just our learners who are not always ready to embrace change as much as we and others would love to see it embraced. Try to master a new tech toy like a recently upgraded smartphone or even a simple piece of office equipment like a photocopier with enhanced features and we quickly become far more empathetic toward our learners.

When we are ready to become more serious about the challenges change presents to all of us in our roles as internal consultants, trainers, teachers, and even learners, we have plenty of resources at our fingertips. A quick search of a library online catalog using the term *change management,* for example, readily produces dozens of options, including the somewhat humbling *Complete Idiot's Guide to Change Management*—not that any of us need to consider ourselves idiots for wanting to engage at any level in the process of change.[16] On the more serious side of the spectrum is Everett Rogers's seminal *The Diffusion of Innovations*—a book as amazing for its comprehensive overview of the topic as it is for the number of ideas that have become standard fare in the area of change management and change facilitation.[17] Those who lack the time or inclination to make their way through this 551-page volume will find serviceable introductions, on Wikipedia, to Rogers and to the overall theme of how change spreads.[18]

BENEFITS AND RISKS OF CONSULTING WITHIN OUR OWN ORGANIZATIONS

If we believe an administrator's promise that the door is always open and that we can walk through that door with a consultant's eye toward innovation and problem resolution and attempt to make use of that offer, we need to be ready for the angry and sometimes explosive reactions from the managers we bypass in attempting to move things to a higher level. Then again, what else should we expect when we are suggesting something that threatens the status quo?

"The paid employee as consultant has to be more mindful of political mine-fields," Jay Turner, training manager for Gwinnett County Public Library, suggests. "I think that you have to be more diplomatic with how you present your viewpoints/findings if they are contrary to what people want to hear. You have to stay as objective as possible, justify everything, communicate through the right channels, and keep your feelings to yourself."

Management can nurture the development of internal consultants, Lee County Library System continuing education coordinator Catherine Vaughn believes:

> First, management must assure the [other] employees that this person is not here to try to find fault, identify mistakes, [and] point out who does what better, but to help the organization grow and to become more efficient. We are looking at processes, not singling out individual behaviors. When the results are announced, it must be presented in that very way. . . . I believe management sets the positive or negative tone of any organization. And I also believe that enough staff are not

recognized for "looking at the big picture" while working. . . . I would like to add that trust needs to be a factor when using an employee to be an internal consultant.

Louise Whitaker, training coordinator for the Pioneer Library System, agrees on the importance of having supportive administrators if trainers-as-leaders are going to function as consultants within their own organizations. Whitaker is able to function as an internal consultant, she says, because "it is recognized that I have a lot to offer; the value is recognized, both from staff and the administration. I guess just the fact that people are willing to ask me, because they know that I'm available to help [encourages her to take on the role of internal consultant]. That's one of the things we've stressed with all staff: if you need someone to help staff a desk, call me. If you need help with training, call me." Her success in this area comes from creating a feeling that she is available, accessible, and willing, she adds.

Conflicts, on the other hand, can develop when paid employees try to serve in this capacity, Whitaker acknowledges: "I think it's more personality-based. Some people have all of the skills, but they just rub someone the wrong way. I've not seen it cause any problems for the organization [Pioneer Library System]. I think it causes problems more on an individual basis than for the organization."

To be effective as a consultant within one's own organization, "one has to be knowledgeable about all aspects of working in the library, from shelving books to intellectual freedom. They have to be accessible, and . . . people have to feel comfortable asking them, knowing that the person is going to help them rather than putting them down," Whitaker concludes.

Sandra Smith echoes this sentiment and explains how she "partners with library managers" so that they see her as a resource to enhance their management skills rather than a competing or conflicting source. She recalls in her first weeks as learning and development manager for Denver Public Library taking each manager out for coffee to chat, explaining what her role was, and establishing good rapport with each manager.

Since leaders are, by definition, instigators of change, and change is what the well ensconced are most averse to seeing, it is no surprise that we can find ourselves in the middle of a conflict when we become part of that process. We then must ask ourselves how far we believe we can go in doing what we think is right for the organization and for all we serve while still being cognizant of and willing to accept the long-term risks we take vis-à-vis our ability to continue functioning effectively within our organizations.

We certainly, as internal consultants, have a level of experience, depth, and understanding of our organization that external consultants simply cannot obtain in the short time given to them when serving as external consultants. If we have been successful in developing the sort of relationships that nurture workplace successes, we understand how to pull the key players—the real change leaders— together to expedite the process we are meant to be facilitating. We also have a level of commitment to the organization and its customers and clients that few external consultants have the luxury of developing—unless they/we are lucky enough to be working with organizations in their own communities.

"We, as trainers, need to remember . . . to have a big picture focus," Smith suggests:

> We need to see the workings of the library from the third-eye. I do this every day [by asking questions such as] "What is the view of the library from the rooftop looking in? What's happening on a daily basis? On a systemic basic? What is the atmosphere people are working in? What's working well? What barriers are there to achievements? What are the needs of the staff collectively? Individually?" . . . We must broaden our viewing lens to see the view from 30,000 feet to be able to see what place our skills can make a difference, and also the path to making that happen. . . . And I'll add that the path we need to take to be successful must be purposefully navigated, with skills, insight, collaboration, good intent, and a bit of luck!

Turner is equally explicit in describing how he approaches his dual role as trainer-as-leader and internal consultant:

> To me, being an internal consultant means that, while I have a high degree of autonomy over how the training function operates, I still work alongside relevant stakeholders to ensure that the organization's training and development needs are met. This allows library administration to articulate what the performance measure should be from the top down, while allowing me to make the roadmap of how we'll get there from the bottom up. I also feel that my input is valued by my peers and superiors if there is a disconnect somewhere in between the two. . . . Taking the consultant role does help further the learning opportunities available to staff, because as the person in the middle between admin and the branches [and] departments, I can distill a pretty clear vision of what the real learning needs (and wants) are. I'm

able to implement a program here at Gwinnett that I think consistently addresses both with a wide variety of opportunities.

In the best of all situations—where external consultants work effectively with staff willing to and capable of functioning as internal consultants, the results are fantastic, our colleagues note. "We have used outside trainers . . . and there was no resentment at all," Janet Hildebrand observes. Members of library staff "could never have spent the time to give every employee in our organization a full day's worth of training, and they have benefited tremendously from the project by having more competent staff to work with and a pool of peer trainers to help design other rollouts with them in technical areas."

What makes that possible at Contra Costa, Hildebrand adds, is

> the kind of leadership we've had from the top for twenty years. . . .
> [County librarian] Anne [Cain] has always led us by example and by
> her direction to her administrative staff that we bring to a project for it
> to be its best, and we ask lots of questions and we consider everything.
> . . . We do not guard, protect, compete. She has always been a person
> who leaves ego outside the door and thinks of questions to ask that don't
> even occur to other people. That's what she expects of everyone. And
> when decisions are made, everyone knows why. So the expectation is
> that we work as a team, and we figure out what is best moving forward.

If we briefly return to the subject of the previous chapter—communities of learning—we can see a natural and wonderful process falling into place. If we are in an organization where strong cohesive communities of learning exist, we have a natural constituency from which to draw. We can seek advice and gain a preliminary sense of whether we are embarking on a challenge worth pursuing or are about to take a lemming-like leap off a cliff with no hope of having a safety net to catch us. The result for everyone involved is a level of achievement and satisfaction upon which other achievements and causes for celebration can be developed.

"I think that it's important for any trainer-as-leader to love wholeheartedly what they do," Turner suggests.

> As a leader, it's important to demonstrate that level of commitment to
> learning or whatever else. If you truly love your enterprise, I think you
> have no other choice than try to act as an internal consultant. So in this
> light, there are no pros and cons—you just have to do it. In exchange
> for potentially having more of a stake and say-so in organizational
> learning, you just have to accept the mantle of additional responsibility
> and subsequent accountability.

Through every action we take in our day-to-day jobs as trainer-learner-leaders, we demonstrate our own knowledge, skills, and aptitude not only in training but in nearly every area of the organization. Pat Wagner says that after a while you "develop a certain kind of expertise that's respected. Then it's pretty easy no matter where you are in the organization for people to respect you."

NOTES

1. Alan Weiss, *Million Dollar Consulting: The Professional's Guide to Growing a Practice,* 3rd ed. (New York: McGraw-Hill, 2003), 4, 37.

2. Peter Block, *Flawless Consulting: A Guide to Getting Your Expertise Used,* 2nd ed. (San Francisco: Jossey-Bass/Pfeiffer, 2000), 27, 2.

3. Ibid., 328–330.

4. Ibid., 338–339.

5. Gordon and Ronald Lippitt, *The Consulting Process in Action,* 2nd ed. (San Diego: University Associates, 1986), 99.

6. On ADDIE, see Elaine Biech (ed.), *The ASTD Handbook for Workplace Learning Professionals* (Alexandria: ASTD Press, 2008), 196–197, 202–210. On ARDDIE, see Benjamin Ruark, "The Year 2013: ARDDIE Is In, ADDIE Is Out," *T+D* 62, no. 7 (2008): 44–49, http://findarticles.com/p/articles/mi_m4467/is_200807/ai_n27996027/. We extend the discussion of ADDIE and ARDDIE in chapter 4.

7. Lippitt and Lippitt, *Consulting Process,* 64.

8. Ibid., 70.

9. Ibid., 74.

10. Block, *Flawless Consulting,* 130.

11. Andrew Jefferson, Roy Pollock, and Calhoun Wick, *Getting Your Money's Worth from Training and Development: A Guide to Breakthrough Learning for Managers* (San Francisco: Pfeiffer: An Imprint of Wiley, 2009); and Jefferson, Pollock, and Wick, *Getting Your Money's Worth from Training and Development: A Guide to Breakthrough Learning for Participants* (San Francisco: Pfeiffer: An Imprint of Wiley, 2009).

12. See Paul Signorelli, "E-learning: Annotated Bibliography for Library Training Programs," 2009, http://paulsignorelli.com/PDFs/E-learning_Annotated_Bibliography_June_2009 .pdf.

13. See Paul Signorelli, "Dynamic Web Conferencing and Presentation Skills for Effective Meetings, Trainings, and Learning Sessions," http://paulsignorelli.com/PDFs/ Bibliography--Webconferencing_Resources.pdf.

14. See Paul Signorelli, "Skype and Low-Cost E-learning Delivered at the Moment of Need," *Building Creative Bridges,* http://buildingcreativebridges.wordpress.com/2010/01/22/ skype-and-low-cost-e-learning-delivered-at-the-moment-of-need/; and "E-learning, Google Chat, and Innovation," *Building Creative Bridges,* http://buildingcreativebridges .wordpress.com/2010/01/13/e-learning-google-chat-and-innovation/.

15. Karen Hyman, "Customer Service and the 'Rule of 1965,'" *American Libraries,* 30, no. 9 (1999): 54–56.

16. Jeffrey Davidson, *The Complete Idiot's Guide to Change Management* (Indianapolis: Alpha, 2002).

17. Everett Rogers, *The Diffusion of Innovations*, 5th ed. (New York: Free Press, 2003).
18. Wikipedia, "Everett Rogers," http://en.wikipedia.org/wiki/Everett_Rogers; and "Diffusion of Innovations," http://en.wikipedia.org/wiki/Diffusion_of_innovations.

4

PREPARING TO DELIVER
FROM INITIAL IDEA TO MOMENT
OF DELIVERY

A learning experience should be as transformative for the
instructor as it is for the participant.

—Pat Wagner, Management Consultant and Trainer

When learning happens in libraries and nonprofit organizations, it often appears akin to magic. The process of developing effective learning, on the other hand, is far from inexplicable, as conversations with workplace learning and performance leaders show. The collaborations, the behind-the-scenes efforts, the planning, unplanning, and replanning can be condensed into amazingly short periods of time or can expand to fill months or even years of available time. What is consistent is that there is a vision to be implemented, and the best among us know how to bring their dreams and visions to fruition.

"I'm a doer and not much of a planner," Gwinnett County Public Library training manager Jay Turner admits without reservation. "After I determine what the learning outcomes should be, I often dive right into constructing the learning experience, and then . . . tinker, tweak, or even get rid of ideas as I flesh out the content. People hate to see my work process, but they are usually satisfied with the end result."

In spite of his caveats about doing rather than planning, Turner, in conversation, proves to be as well organized and as thoughtful about the learning process as everyone else interviewed for this book. As he prepares for a new classroom-based or online learning session, he begins by identifying what he expects from learners after they have left the physical or virtual classroom, then writes course objectives and begins preparing a formal lesson plan. He determines the mode of delivery, then chooses a teaching technique along with strategies to use during the formal presentation. He also considers the location and room arrangements for the session based on discussions with colleagues and on the session activities he is planning.

"If I decide online delivery is better, I then determine if it will be synchronous or asynchronous, at which point I'm back to rethinking my teaching delivery," he notes. "I don't keep a hard and fast template but, rather, follow this process mentally. I do have a couple of checklists to help me handle logistics before I go live."

Some of the best workplace learning and performance leaders we have seen appear to view leadership as involving listening as much as initiating actions. During their first weeks or months on the job, they work to meet immediate needs while also visiting staff in the various facilities throughout the organizations they serve; become active on committees that are directly or indirectly involved in the delivery of learning opportunities; spend as much time outside their offices as they do inside them so they can hear what colleagues value, need, and want from the learning and performance program; and attend some of the organization's current offerings to see how they are delivered, received, and meeting the overall mission, vision, and value statements adopted by the organizations they now are serving. They also contact colleagues in other local or regional library systems or nonprofit organizations to determine what is being done elsewhere, and many become active participants in online synchronous and asynchronous discussion groups to keep track of available resources, developing trends, and opportunities for collaboration beyond the walls of their own buildings—a topic explored in greater depth in the final chapter of this book.

When Turner became the training manager at Gwinnett County Public Library, he spent much of his first year "just learning the managerial aspect of the position and not straying too far from the status quo." "Now," he recalls, "after having soaked it all in, I have developed a yearly training plan based on a needs analysis and will focus on categories of need by the quarter."

Peter Bromberg, while working for the South Jersey Regional Library Cooperative, was equally goal driven in that agency, which offered approximately fifty workshops per year before closing due to budget cuts in 2010. "My end goal [was] that if anyone walks into any library in the southern seven counties of New Jersey or accesses any services remotely, they have the best possible experience. Great service. Great resources. Great environment. Great experience," he said. "I then work[ed] backwards and ask[ed] myself, and the libraries, 'What skills, abilities, and resources do the library staff need to deliver that experience?'"

Bromberg follows a process similar to that described by Turner, including working with instructors to develop workshops effectively, and also becomes involved in marketing efforts to be sure that offerings and learners are matched. Part of his leadership involved watching for topics that had not yet been requested but clearly met a need in the cooperative. "These classes tend to be on the edge of awareness," he notes. "No one ever asked for those classes, but once they're scheduled, they fill immediately and people ask for more. . . . That comes from just paying attention to what's going on in the world and listening to conversations over lunch about what challenges and frustrations library staff are experiencing, or even simply what they're curious about."

Other sources of information for Bromberg include blogs such as the ALA Learning Round Table's *ALA Learning,* Michelle Martin's *The Bamboo Project,* and the *Library Garden* blog to which Bromberg contributed through August 2010.[1]

Many workplace learning and performance professionals themselves note that developing procedures, checklists, and templates is far from a one-time task. At the Pioneer Library System, training coordinator Louise Whitaker was updating everything when we spoke during summer 2009: "We're in the process of moving toward developing online tutorials for our databases and technical skills, our soft skills, and we're going to be using WebEx for synchronous trainings," she noted. "In developing these new trainings, we're looking at our training objectives, the WebJunction core competencies, and using templates so that the trainings will cover the same components."

The introduction of online learning opportunities actually led her to create standardized procedures where none had existed: "We had training objectives for each course; we're trying to be more intentional as we take this next step. Also, I am working with a training advisory group with people from other branches. Their input into the training program is important because it brings a different perspective."

Denver Public Library learning and development manager Sandra Smith, like her colleagues, uses formal and informal checklists to complete needs assessments when she begins the planning process. This helps her identify outcomes and measure and evaluate the results of what is offered to staff within the library system. "I always keep those in mind as I do the most important thing, which is to talk to the stakeholders and learn what they need and how we might make it happen together in planning. . . . I have eighty-plus staff people who are willing to share their expertise and passion and do this with limited time."

Her leadership role in this process has included making colleagues aware of the library's long-standing commitment to training, which dates back to the days when John Cotton Dana was director. "In finding out this wonderful history,

I realized that one of my biggest accomplishments has been to renew and recharge staff's awareness and appreciation of the importance and relevance of our being skilled and knowledgeable. We are newly upholding the great learning tradition of the staff at DPL."

Pat Wagner, who has been consulting and providing learning opportunities for the staffs of libraries throughout the United States for more than three decades, has also drawn from old and new educational models:

> There are over fifty major theories of how people learn. During and since college, I have studied many of them. Having [also] been a college instructor at five different universities and colleges over a decade really taught me a lot about adult education. . . . one measure I always make of a successful class is [that] I should be learning every time I step into a classroom or do online training. A learning experience should be as transformative for the instructor as it is for the participant.

Determining what needs to be offered in training begins early in the planning process through the simple act of asking specific questions, Wagner says: "How will learners' workplace behavior differ as a result of what they learn, and what concrete (rather than abstract) nouns will describe the behavior of those who attend learning sessions?" She also tries to determine whether what is needed is even something that can be accomplished through training, or whether the issue is more one of an employee or group of employees in need of more effective supervision. "What will be the physical evidence that my program has been successful? What will you see and hear that makes you glad someone went to that session? You would be surprised how many times a client can't answer that question," she notes.

In assessing the need for any particular learning opportunity, workplace learning and performance professionals need to gather information in a variety of ways and from a variety of sources, Wagner maintains: "What people tell you on a survey online is different than what they say if their boss is in the room. . . . I had six cancellations last month despite the director asking and people saying, 'yes, we need this.' They were still cancelled because of low enrollment. Conducting proper assessments is no guarantee. In effect, there is no guarantee, and that's something that people have to understand."

"Trainers are asked to solve problems that are not training problems," she also notes. "The majority of training issues could be solved if supervisors did their jobs"—a point that leads her to suggest that "most training should be done by supervisors." Trying to resolve supervisory issues with inappropriate training, she continues, can actually be demoralizing and lead to wasted time—particularly if an organization mandates training for all employees when the issue to be resolved involves a much smaller group.

"Supervisors need to be good at this [managing performance and employee evaluations]; it is not optional," Contra Costa County Library deputy county librarian Janet Hildebrand agreed in a separate interview. "The supervisor isn't always the one who does the training, but the supervisor must recognize that training is always part of the plan for developing performance, for taking great employees to the next level, for giving poorer employees the possibility for reaching success, and for dealing with employees who won't improve." Because the supervisors' role in workplace learning and performance is considered so important at Contra Costa, system administrators have designed one of the most comprehensive training programs for community library managers that we have seen. Among the nearly two dozen topics included in the orientation plan are staff training and staff development; the strategic plan and role of community libraries; separate sessions on the relationship with the city, with Friends organizations, and with the library commission and city library commissioner; staffing; the volunteer program; collection development; performance evaluations; and the hiring process.

The Contra Costa new employee training program is also among the most rigorous we have encountered. Continuing over a four-week period with more than fifteen peer trainers involved, it integrates classroom training and hands-on practice; provides orientations to all departments and service programs; includes background on the governance, history, and operations of the library; instills an understanding of library policies; and emphasizes excellent customer service.

"Leaders lead by offering a learning hand to the staff who will take it and run, and there are always staff to be found in that category," Hildebrand maintains. "Even if in the beginning they are in the minority, we invest our energy and our emotions on those and don't focus our attention on the most resistant and negative." Those who do not pass the four-week new staff orientation are simply not hired, she notes.

ADDIE AND ARDDIE

One much discussed instructional design tool is the ADDIE model—an acronym for "analysis, design, development, implementation, and evaluation"—which provides structure from start to finish for face-to-face as well as online learning opportunities. It clearly reflects much of what workplace learning and development leaders tell us as they discuss their own approaches to the work they do, and it is a model heavily promoted by ASTD.

As if to support what Louise Whitaker and others say about the need to adapt new tools to match changing workplace learning and performance circumstances, ASTD has been introducing an updated version—ARDDIE—which adds research into the mix.[2] The suggestion that evidence-based research should be an integral part of the planning process for learning opportunities may be news to many current practitioners, but students currently earning their MLS/MLIS degrees are leaving school firmly rooted in that process since their instructors so often stress the need for that level of work as students move out of school and into the library workplace. As these new graduates—many of whom already have experience working in libraries before earning their degrees—assume increasing amounts of leadership opportunities and as training becomes part of their day-to-day work with colleagues as well as with library members and guests, we may see an increased use of research that supports effective learning and relies more on results that can be documented rather than on anecdotes that may or may not be leading instructors to provide learning opportunities that produce long-term, sustainable, and verifiable results. In the meantime, leaders in library and nonprofit workplace learning and performance programs continue working at the large level of coordinating annual training plans that produce effective and continually evolving individual learning opportunities.

THE TRAINING PLAN

Like Contra Costa County Library's training programs for new employees and community library managers, the overall training plan for the Charlotte Mecklenburg Library aims to be comprehensive, and employees who do not complete the program face repercussions, including lower performance evaluation ratings (see the appendix to this volume). Designed to help all staff members develop their existing skills and talents and to provide them with a well-outlined path for their professional development, it includes courses that assist in the development and strengthening of several core competencies: customer service, communication, safety and security, programming, readers' advisory, technology skills, and use of the organization's integrated library system. Courses are offered through a variety of sources including the library's human resources department and the Mecklenburg County Learning Services Department. It projects a combination of face-to-face, online, and blended learning opportunities.

The program continues, during employees' first three months at the library, with short introductions on how to take advantage of the library's learning and development program and how to learn online; a variety of offerings about how to use workplace digital tools and more integrated library system coursework; separate sessions on how to work with children and how to work with teens; and two-hour courses on how to locate events happening throughout the library system and how to register library members and guests for those events.

By the time employees have been with the library for six months, they are also expected to have completed separate readers' advisory sessions concentrating on basics, then youth, then adults; and sessions on reference skills, including how to conduct effective reference interviews.

The remaining months of the employees' first year on the job include coursework on how to market the library's collections effectively; how to work with library volunteers; preventing sexual harassment in the workplace; and nonviolent crisis intervention. Supplemental courses include basics of training design and presentation skills.

Training plans within other organizations vary in their design and complexity. For example, the San Francisco Public Library system, over a decade-long period, went from having no formal staff training program to an interim step of having one with offerings from a few different providers on a limited number of topics and with a goal of training everyone on specific issues before considering that training completed and moving on to other equally large topics. The program continued to evolve. It combined previous elements by drawing from an increasingly varied number of providers to facilitate training on an as-needed basis and occasionally focusing on system-wide issues such as the need for ergonomic training for those who used computer equipment or who were involved in heavy lifting and bending, or system-wide training as a new integrated library system replaced what had been used. The largest shift occurred when those one-time system-wide efforts began including follow-up courses at two levels: courses for newly hired staff who missed the one-time system-wide offerings, and ongoing courses for those in need of updates or for specialized offerings.

The result was an organized program that provided approximately fifty learning opportunities face-to-face or online every quarter, publicized through a formal printed catalog distributed throughout the main library and each of the twenty-seven branch libraries and also posted online on the staff intranet. New offerings took the place of sessions that were no longer needed through a process that created a program responsive to current needs. The planning process itself was deliberately simple: an Excel spreadsheet listed courses by category including general, supervisory, computer-based, and health and safety; the spreadsheet was updated at the end of each quarter so that there was always a yearlong plan in place that could easily be altered to meet unexpected needs.

More comprehensive software is also in use, as Catherine Vaughn and her colleagues in the Lee County Library system show through their use of Compliance Suite. Following the same basic pattern used in San Francisco, Vaughn reviews and updates the library training plan throughout the year; works with her supervisor, branch managers, and other key staff to remain cognizant of newly developing needs; and tracks what is happening through the software.

> Each employee has a log-in so they can schedule, unschedule, and check the calendar for upcoming classes. It takes the burden off me because I used to schedule everyone for every session staff members attended. . . . The exception to this system is our library cooperative classes. Staff register themselves and then report their attendance to me in a monthly report so it is recorded in the database for an accurate education history. Staff can also check their history to make sure something isn't missing. Supervisors can log in to see all of the staff who report to them to aid in the evaluation process.

The result clearly is the creation and support of a community of learners where everyone takes part in the organization's continuing education needs.

Sandra Smith uses similar procedures with a less automated system at Denver Public:

> The DPL training calendar and TRACKS (Training Resources and Continuing Knowledge for Staff) newsletter are published three times a year. Over seventy sessions are offered to staff in each, ranging from technical to soft skills to workplace awareness and coping to new customer needs. TRACKS has brief articles on what's new, what's up in learning, my perspective on what's affecting staff at the moment, and anything else that might motivate or be interesting to staff to get them thinking about learning.

This system also obviously serves as part of a continually evolving annual plan that combines core, repeating courses with new offerings scheduled as quickly as they can be designed and produced. "The calendar is an online product, but not yet an LMS," she adds. "And by the way, our volunteers, docents, and substitute staff are welcome to attend classes."

The Charlotte Mecklenburg Library has moved away from newsletter formats for keeping staff up-to-date in learning news and instead relies heavily on the staff news portion of its Drupal-based intranet. The ability to use blogs and other media where anyone can create and post online content has revolutionized the world of information. These new tools do, however, have ironic consequences. Where once we could not get information out fast enough, we are now in a position where members of staff are receiving too much information, so much so that requests are coming in to trainers around the country on how to keep up with news and information.

I'M OK, YOU'RE STRESSED OUT

Among the elements workplace learning and performance leaders consistently examine is the overall environment in which learning opportunities are delivered. They recognize, for good reason, that a less than accommodating setting and set of circumstances in which to learn produce less than stellar results, and if anything about the delivery of the lesson induces stress, they know they might as well dismiss the class and take a very long lunch break. Since personal involvement goes a long way in producing memorable and effective learning experiences, let's take a look at an extreme example of how learning can go wrong in a far from ideal situation.

A group of us who were enrolled in an introductory leadership course had less than a week to coalesce as highly functioning collaborative units, tackle an ill-defined project together, and produce a tangible product. We were, early in that first week together, broken into three teams, given broad project descriptions, and then given a few days to struggle with team dynamics, the challenge of mastering complex new material, and the need to determine exactly what needed to be learned and what needed to be done. Since no one was at any point very clear on what the final product should be, each team struggled with the challenge and the accompanying stress, with different results: one team completely divorced itself from the other two and worked on its own throughout the week whenever we were not together in the shared classroom; a second team attempted to interact with members of the other teams whenever possible inside and outside the classroom setting; and the third team was so overwhelmed by the stress of the assignment that one member actually walked out on colleagues in tears for nearly an hour during one group meeting and, upon returning, worked independently of the others or solely with one other member and repeatedly missed deadlines. The team that attempted to interact with others finished their project by 8 p.m. the night before the assignment was due; the team that worked completely away from the other two also finished its work that evening. The team that was overcome by the stress of the ambiguous assignment was still working to complete the assignment at midnight that night, and final copies for their completed project were printed off just a few hours before the deadline.

When the 9 a.m. deadline arrived, there was no time to rest on laurels or celebrate successes—a key component of successful team building, as Joan Giesecke and Beth McNeil write: "Celebrate the unit's completion of tasks and projects in order to thank staff for their hard work and to reinforce the benefits of planning."[3] Having submitted the completed projects, members of each of the three teams were already facing the challenge of having an hour-long seminar ready for presentation to their instructors and colleagues four days later.

There was, however, an unexpectedly great learning opportunity provided by the instructors at the end of the first week. Asking how we had reacted to the initial assignment and what we had learned, they were greeted by an hour-long, no-holds-barred discussion of what was good and what was not good about the initial experience of completing a massive project within newly formed teams of students/leaders-in-training under extremely stressful circumstances. We were very direct in expressing deep concerns over how the project was handled and the overall way material was presented; to their credit, the instructors listened rather than reacted during the initial part of this discussion, and they did all they apparently could do for the remainder of the three-week program to respond creatively and positively to what they heard. This did not resolve all of the issues raised during that in-class discussion, but it did provide a level of support that helped members of at least one of the teams function better within the continuing constraints and stress created and imposed by the structure of that leadership course.

What was true at that moment and remained true throughout the course was that those students who fell into the trap of skipping meals, sleeping only a few hours each night, and failing to carve out time to reflect upon lessons learned and lessons to be learned were more prone to withdraw from collaborative efforts than those who established schedules that included time for breaks, meals, reflection, and longer amounts of sleep. They expressed frustration with their own work and with their teammates, repeatedly complained of the high stress levels they were experiencing, and, in extreme cases, yelled at colleagues and again broke down in tears.

These demonstrations of low-quality work-group-level efforts as opposed to high-performance-team results served as evidence of what research by Charlotte Shelton, Mindi McKenna, and John Darling suggests: "Stress and urgency . . . inhibit the functioning of the neo-cortex. Creative breakthroughs rarely occur during periods of high anxiety. Therefore, leaders who wish to become quantum [creatively effective] thinkers first must learn to manage stress."[4]

Warren Bennis notes that it "is the individual, operating at the peak of his creative and moral powers, who will revive our organizations, by reinventing himself and them." He also writes, "Because reflection is vital—at every level, in every organization—and because burnout is a very real threat in today's hectic atmosphere, all executives should practice the new three Rs: retreat, renewal, and return."[5]

Malcolm Knowles, Elwood Holton III, and Richard Swanson have written at great length about the importance of a supportive learning environment in which adult learners have clearly defined assignments and low levels of stress. In one key section, they offer the following summary of evidence-based research:

> Cognitive theorists stress the importance of a psychological climate of orderliness, clearly defined goals, careful explanation of expectations and opportunities, openness of the system to inspection and questioning, and honest and objective feedback. . . . Personality theorists . . . emphasize the importance of a climate in which . . . anxiety levels are appropriately controlled (enough to motivate but not so much as to block). . . . They prescribe a "mentally healthful" climate.[6]

John Dirkx provides an overview worth quoting at length for anyone still in doubt about what is needed for successful adult learning to occur:

> The literature underscores the importance of attending to emotions and feelings in contexts, interactions, and relationships that characterize adult learning (Boud, Cohen, and Walker, 1993; Brookfield, 1993; Daloz, 1986; Postle, 1993; Robertson, 1996; Tennant, 1997). A growing body of research, however, suggests that emotions and feelings are more than merely a motivational concern in learning. Postle (1993) argues that affective, emotional dimensions provide the foundation on which practical, conceptual, and imaginal modes of learning rest. "Brain-based" theories (Damasio, 1994, 1999) and the concept of "emotional intelligence" (Goleman, 1995) suggest that emotion and feelings are deeply interrelated with perceiving and processing information from our external environments, storing and retrieving information in memory, reasoning, and the embodiment of learning (Merriam and Caffarella, 1999; Taylor, 1996). Recent studies of transformative learning reveal extrarational aspects, such as emotion, intuition, soul, spirituality, and the body, as integral to processes of deep, significant change (Clark, 1997; Dirkx, 1997; Nelson, 1997; Scott, 1997).[7]

All of this points out a terrible and still unresolved problem in the way that leadership course was delivered:

If the leaders-in-training within the classrooms are intentionally subjected to intense stress (which inhibits learning) right at the moment when they should be learning how to control their stress, and

if everything we know from research, peer-reviewed journals, well respected writers' books, and our own experience about what is necessary for successful learning—and, by extension, successful team-building—shows that stress inhibits learning,

then what sort of leader does a program like that produce? And how many potentially great leaders will be diverted to other pursuits because they left the program and the field as a result of what they experienced through that course?

SETTING THE STAGE

We were lucky, in the course of conducting interviews for this book, to find workplace learning and performance professionals who repeatedly emphasized the importance of creating supportive, creative, and inviting environments for those who turned to them for help. It was not uncommon for us, during our conversations, to talk about the importance of providing a comfortable classroom for onsite learning and support to online learners who were new to e-learning.

Setting the virtual or face-to-face stage is a critically important element in producing learning opportunities that produce positive effects, we agreed during those conversations. Whenever we have control over the spaces in which we and other instructors work, we become the architects who create spaces we ourselves would love to inhabit because we know those are the spaces that produce training-teaching-learning capable of delivering what it promises: positive change benefiting individuals and the organizations and customers they serve.

The importance of being attentive to detail was not lost during those conversations. We know that how we set up the chairs within a room or how the virtual learning environment appears in e-learning creates an immediate impression that contributes to or alleviates stress. If a classroom or workshop setting does not look right when we walk in—preferably 30–45 minutes before the session is scheduled to begin—we seek help or actually rearrange the room ourselves to do whatever is possible to improve the setup.

A basic question tends to be posed at every possible moment: what can be done to make the setting and the lesson engaging? We remember that in our earliest learning experiences, in preschool or kindergarten settings, learning was fun, and then it started to become a little more serious and competitive, and fun somehow seemed to disappear from the equation. We note that, although we are used to thinking of training and learning centers as having plenty of ergonomically correct chairs placed in carefully measured rows in front of state-of-the-art computer screens, we are encouraged to see some of our favorite trainer-teacher-learners managing to capture a little of the fun so many others have left behind; they have playful objects that encourage interaction and creativity—the keys to building even short-term communities of learning—on tables during workplace learning and performance activities so that participants can remain engaged yet not lose track of what presenters are offering.

We know that making learners comfortable from the moment they enter the workshop setting makes them allies instead of adversaries, so we do everything we can to show them that we care enough about them to think about how they feel, to lay the groundwork for a level of engagement that takes them to the next level of coalescing into learning groups. We are prepared to greet them at the door and chat informally to gather information about what they expect to learn and what has motivated them to arrive for that particular learning session. Whenever we have the budget to do so, we provide simple beverages and food; we recognize that we need not produce anything elaborate, but we also recognize that it is worth fighting for a refreshment budget if we are involved in a workplace learning and performance setting where colleagues return for sessions and see each other often enough actually to develop that all-important community of learners we are seeking to nurture and sustain.

The room temperature where the learning opportunity is offered is also important. This sometimes is the hardest element for us to control since so many buildings have automated or building-wide temperature control units. It is what we could call the Goldilocks' Porridge Syndrome: one is too hot, one is too cold, and one is just right. If we, or those who control the settings, fail to keep things comfortable, we cannot be too surprised if we find ourselves facing a somewhat bearlike audience. Something to consider when we have any level of control over the heating or cooling system within a room: it is worth asking how those sitting around us or in front of us are feeling, and seeing if we can reach someone to adjust the temperature as needed. And remember that we are likely to be much warmer than they are because we are moving around a bit—or a lot. Seeing people wearing parkas or wrapping scarves around their necks might be an early warning sign.

A final consideration for workplace learning and performance leaders involves the quality of sound in the room where sessions are offered. This is more than just checking the volume on the microphone. If we have a partner or an early arrival who is willing to assist, we can test the microphone—using it ourselves and then walking around the room to gauge the sound when someone else is using it—and then walk around to see how sound carries throughout the room even without amplification. And it is well worth listening for dead zones—areas where sound suddenly drops off because it is absorbed by some sort of overhang or other acoustical obstacle within the room. There is not much we can do about some of the sound problems, but being aware of them allows us to warn audience members ahead of time and gives us the ability to compensate for those problems we cannot fix.

All of these elements lead us to a somewhat obvious if unexpected conclusion: presentation is about the senses and how we use them. If we take those senses into consideration as we plan our presentations and set the stage, and if we make ourselves aware of how our own senses are in use as we check out the setting we are about to use, we are giving ourselves another wonderful tool to provide our audience with memorable experiences, and we are doing everything possible to reduce the stress that can ruin the effectiveness of the best-prepared lessons.

PREPARATION, REHEARSAL, AND DRESS REHEARSAL

As we consider all that goes into preparation for the day of delivering a learning opportunity, we cannot avoid the importance of rehearsal. The North Carolina Certified Training Specialist program provided to government workers by the North Carolina Office of State Personnel teaches participants to "choose when you are going to sweat"—you can sweat before a training session with hard work and preparation, or you can sweat during a training session as you discover the consequences of being unprepared.

"So much of what's important—most of it, I'd argue—is done before the actual training—the planning, the prep work, the thinking through, the instructional design," Peter Bromberg notes. "By the time I get to the actual training, that's mostly cake!"

Part of the preparation for a training session, whether face-to-face or online, should be one or more informal practice sessions or formal rehearsals either in private or as a pilot session with a small group of participants who can provide constructive criticism. The importance of run-throughs in front of a small audience cannot be emphasized enough. Often we become so immersed in the finer details of creating the training that we miss the bigger picture of providing a context for our learners or using analogies to tie pieces together.

Furthermore, because public speaking is "the No. 1 fear reported by people in the U.S." and that fear may actually be an innate trait, a 2006 communications study by Paul L. Witt suggests, preparation and rehearsal can be among the best tools we have for managing that fear.[8]

A dress rehearsal for a trainer means running through the presentation using the same equipment in the same location in which the training will be delivered. This helps us avoid credibility-draining experiences such as arriving to deliver a class on Web 2.0 technology and discovering, in those final moments before the session is scheduled to begin, that wireless Internet access is turned off for the day because the building is closed to the public.

"I practice, practice, practice, practice, practice—however many times you want to print that word out—so I can effectively deliver the material," Pat Wagner says. "For every hour I stand in front of a class, I practice one hundred hours." She also prepares a script before delivering a presentation for the first time, although she never reads from it during the class. "That doesn't mean I memorize every word, but it means I'm prepared to deliver the lesson," she says.

Maurice Coleman, in an ALA Learning blog post, discusses his "BGIMD [Bald Geek in Maryland] Basic Training Technology Survival Kit," which contains things such as a network cable, extension cord, batteries, even a change of clothes.[9]

Another way of dealing with that fear—in essence, stage fright—is to remember that the learners, in normal circumstances, are collaborators, not adversaries. If we attempt to exert too much control in a classroom—what one colleague refers to as forbidding "solo hiking" by those who want to explore learning paths that might not be in an instructor's lesson plan or overall repertoire—or if we avoid responding to unanticipated questions and concerns learners raise, we may actually limit rather than enhance the chance for success in learning.

"When you are the instructor for a session, you can change the learning climate," Catherine Vaughn says. "You are also seen as the authority on the topic you are delivering. Be ready for all kinds of questions, and never let them see you become unnerved." She continues:

> I was teaching a class on Business Etiquette—this class has given me the best experiences for handling all types of challenges—and we were discussing dress guidelines. Since undergarments were not listed as proper attire, I had a young woman ask in class, "Is it required to wear a bra to work, since it is not on the list?"
>
> Well, I have to say I was *not* ready for that question, and by the looks of the stunned faces of other attendees, they were not expecting it, either. I did, though, reply, looking directly at her and said, "That is a good question. I would answer that by looking at this from the professional standpoint. If I did not wear a bra to work, would I look

and/or feel professional? If the answer is no, than I would say, yes, a bra or some support undergarment for women is required to give you the professional look we are striving for."

LEADERS DREAMING

What is also obvious from conversations with our colleagues is that planning never stops. Whether it involves lunchtime conversations, reading blogs, or talking with and especially listening to coworkers, the best workplace learning and performance leaders are always open to ideas for the next learning opportunity they need to oversee, and they work hard to avoid being hindered by obstacles.

Jay Turner, for example, faced the challenge of wanting to continue an on-again off-again tradition of providing an annual staff development day at Gwinnett County Public Library even though budgetary constraints were threatening his ability to proceed. His solution was to use the library learning management system to host an abbreviated (30-minute) virtual presentation created with tools including Adobe Articulate and Captivate. "It included a state of the library podcast/slideshow from the executive director and various awards presentations delivered by video. I concluded with a virtual raffle ticket system to give out door prizes that were delivered by courier to the branches," he explained.

Asked to dream about how he would create an entire day of online offerings for a staff development day if he had unlimited resources, he quickly outlined a presentation that would take place in a 3-D virtual world "delivered via thin client—no software download—where each staff member has an avatar." The staff development day world would comprise a series of rooms, including "a lounge where everyone can hang out and chat. The lounge is a hub that joins together all the other rooms." Separate virtual rooms would provide settings for breakout sessions or presentations supporting the theme of that particular staff development day. "Staff day would be a week-long event that people could visit at their leisure and hop in and out as they saw fit. I'd have discussion boards enabled in the LMS for staff members to continue conversations about the presentation/breakout sessions."

When we teasingly suggested that he pursue a grant to fund that dream project, Turner offered an unorthodox response that goes to the heart of his leadership and creative talents: "A grant would be good, but I'm sure I could make a go of it with just some free time. I have a knack for creating products with free resources."

NOTES

1. *ALA Learning,* http://alalearning.org/; Michelle Martin, *The Bamboo Project,* http://michelemartin.typepad.com/; *Library Garden,* http://librarygarden.net/.
2. Benjamin Ruark, "Year 2013: ARDDIE Is In, ADDIE Is Out, *T+D* 62, no. 7 (July 2008): 44–49, http://findarticles.com/p/articles/mi_m4467/is_200807/ai_n27996027/.
3. Joan Giesecke and Beth McNeil, *Fundamentals of Library Supervision* (Chicago: American Library Association, 2005), 112.
4. Charlotte Shelton, Mindi McKenna, and John Darling, "Leading in the Age of Paradox: Optimizing Behavioral Style, Job Fit and Cultural Cohesion, *Leadership and Organization Development Journal* 23, no. 7 (2002): 372–379.
5. Warren Bennis, *On Becoming a Leader* (Reading: Addison-Wesley, 1989), 102, 187.
6. Malcolm Knowles, Elwood Holton, and Richard Swanson, *The Adult Learner,* 6th ed. (Burlington, Vt.: Elsevier, 2005), 120.
7. John Dirkx, "The Power of Feelings: Emotion, Imagination, and the Construction of Meaning in Adult Learning," *New Directions for Adult and Continuing Education: The New Update on Adult Learning Theory* 89 (2001): 68.
8. This according to Daniel DeNoon, "Fear of Public Speaking Hardwired," *WebMD,* April 20, 2006, www.webmd.com/anxiety-panic/guide/20061101/fear-public-speaking.
9. Maurice Coleman, "5 Tips for Trainers to Prevent TechFail," *ALA Learning,* http://alalearning.org/2010/02/04/5-tips-for-trainers-to-prevent-techfail/.

5

IN THE MIDDLE
TRAINERS AS LEADERS
IN THE CLASSROOM

You really are a sherpa to get people from . . . where they are to the learning objectives. It's your job to use whatever tools you have to get people from where they are to where they need to be.

—Maurice Coleman, Technical Trainer, Harford County Public Library

S uccess in workplace learning and performance means that learning never stops—and that applies to trainer-teachers as well as to students, particularly on the day when learning opportunities are delivered. The intense levels of preparation we describe in chapter 4 continue on the day training takes place—and beyond—because what we do is cumulative; lessons delivered and lessons learned become part of our repertoire for all the sessions we still have not delivered. If something goes wrong today, we resolve it and remember next time to take steps that avoid a similar disruption in the learning process.

There are mechanical elements to be acknowledged: when we enter a classroom, meeting room, or online environment where we are joining learners, we have with us the tools and resources that come from completing a needs analysis, research, and course objectives and learning outcomes. We also have a degree of self-confidence gained by doing everything possible to draw from our knowledge of adult learning theory and to use instructional methods that can appeal to people with a variety of learning styles. Learning is not a one-size-fits-all endeavor for those in libraries, nonprofits, or any other organization.

If we are really at the top of our game—and who among us would want to admit to any less, even though we know we will have our good days, our bad days, and our really bad days?—we are prepared for everything we can possibly antici-pate. If we are using PowerPoint slides, we have a printout of those slides in case we face technical problems during our presentation. If we have speaker notes—and why wouldn't we when PowerPoint makes it so easy to incorporate them into our presentations?—we have used the "notes page" format to print out our entire presentation so that each sheet of paper has the slide at the top of the page and our notes directly under that slide. If we are drawing from shared document files online, we have copies of those files on a flash drive. If we want learners interact-ing by sitting at small round tables while we are conducting the training sessions, we arrive early enough to be sure that round tables were, in fact, delivered and set up in the pattern we requested—and if they are not, we either help to make things right before the learners arrive or we draw learners into the process of resetting the room in a way that makes them comfortable and likely to be ready to absorb what we are offering.

When we are engaging in online learning, we have just as many elements to consider. We have to be sure, several days in advance, that we have given our producers everything we are going to use. We do not make last-minute changes that would interfere with a producer's ability to serve us and our learners well. If we are using VoIP or calling in via landline, we have tested our tech tools through a rehearsal and also arrive early enough to engage in last-minute troubleshoot-ing with our online collaborators to assure that learners have a chance to learn without having to struggle with those elements of technology that should serve rather than hinder their efforts. There will, we all know, be plenty of unexpected technological challenges to overcome, so we want to avoid adding to the chal-lenges by not anticipating and resolving the easy ones before our sessions begin. We also, if possible, have a second computer nearby and ready to use in case our primary equipment fails during a live presentation.

Some colleagues have checklists to help assure that everything is in place in the physical or virtual classroom; others have checklists of what learners should do before arriving to best prepare themselves for an effec-tive learning experience. Regardless of what we use or do not use, we have a responsibility to our learners, to the colleagues who are allowing them to participate in what we are providing, to the overall organization itself, and, equally important, to the customers who are served by what our students learn.

With so much at stake, there is more than a little irony that so many nonprofit and library trainers—so many of us—have taken or been assigned to positions of responsibility in workplace learning and performance without any formal educa-tion or training on the subject of adult learning; many of us found ourselves in training positions simply because we appeared to be good at explaining things to our coworkers or because no one else was available to plan, schedule, and deliver training. It is this trial-by-fire method of essentially being thrown onto the stage that often teaches us our greatest lessons and gives us examples of what to do and what not to do in the classroom. Trainers often acquire this knowledge after having been in the classroom for a while. Fortunately, for all involved, we have passion and a love for learning, so we acquire these new concepts and skills with ease and readily apply them to the benefit of those who rely on us for help.

THE SHOW MUST GO ON

If we accept that trainers are performers at heart, we have a tremendously positive launching point for success in that performers understand that they cannot stop what they have promised to deliver. If our technology fails us, we acknowledge the failure and proceed with the learning experience to the best of our abilities; only in those rare situations where the technology is an integral part of the learning process and cannot be excluded from successful learning do we accept the inevitable, cancel the session so that learners can use their time more effectively, and return to the lesson when the problem has been rectified. If materials meant to be used in the session are not delivered as planned, we use the backup copy or copies we carried with us and adapt the way we are presenting the material to respond positively to the changed circumstances. If there has been a personal tragedy within the organization where we are working, we do not ignore it and pretend that successful learning can occur while learners are emotionally troubled; we acknowledge the situation, offer learners a few minutes to engage in any level of conversation that helps them process the personal pain they are feeling, and proceed if and when they are composed enough to have a positive and productive leaning experience.

TEACHER-CENTRIC AND LEARNER-CENTRIC TRAINING

One of the more interesting discussions continuing to take place among trainer-teacher-learners is focused on the perception that we are moving from teacher-centric to learner-centric physical and online offerings. The conversation seems to come from the extreme and inaccurate view that education has always been a one-way process, where teachers stand in the front of a group of students and those students absorb as if they were sponges with limitless capacities for expansion; the extreme opposite view, which is equally inaccurate, seems to come from the idea that teacher-trainer-learners are present only to facilitate the learning process and that, if learners do not gain what they are meant to gain, they are to blame for the learning failures that follow.

As with many other ideas we are proposing and documenting here, this particular either/or option seems most easily resolved at some sort of flexible middle point. Those of us delivering training-learning opportunities have a leader's responsibility to determine what must be learned; to ensure that there is sufficient agreement, between the learners and those providing them with the learning opportunities, that the training session can deliver what is needed; and to prepare a workplace situation that will continue to support and nurture returning learners. If magic occurs in physical and virtual learning environments, it is not often going to come from a captive audience of students being bludgeoned into submission by trainers they may see only once or twice; it is going to come from the active participation of trainers, teachers, and learners who come together briefly or for more extended periods to form the sort of learning communities we are describing throughout this book.

Though workplace learning and performance professionals have many opportunities to work as leaders, the classroom—face-to-face or online—is the place where leadership skills are the most visible. "While I'm delivering training online or in-person within my organization, I'm constantly thinking that my role as a leader is to set the sterling example of how things are supposed to be," Gwinnett County Public Library training manager Jay Turner admits.

> For example, if I'm teaching something process-oriented, I do all I can to verify, with subject matter experts, that my steps are correct. If I'm delivering conceptual information for general learning and professional development, I like to challenge learners to think about how they can use those ideas here in the organization to make things better. . . . Finally, regardless of content, I really try to reinforce the library's vision of inspiring, enriching, and amazing—whether it's through my attitude or the approach I take in delivering the content.

Catherine Vaughn, continuing education coordinator for the Lee County Library System, says, "I see myself in an important leadership role. I set the tone. People are watching what I do, listening to what I say and, hopefully, will take away a new thought, idea, or concept to implement. I literally influence the climate [and] culture of an organization." She acknowledges that much of what we see in training-teaching-learning is driven by a desire simply to cover the material included in a lesson plan, getting as many people through sessions as possible, and not paying attention to what happens next. There are, she suggests, ways to avoid that trap:

> I first try to get buy-in from the participants even if they have been told they *must* be in attendance. I then get them excited about what we will be discussing in today's session. We also talk about what they want to discuss, what they want to get from the session, and what they don't want to do. . . . For example: if I tell them we will have some role-playing, and then someone says they don't like to role-play, I will ask them if they have another way to reinforce the concept. I take their suggestion and try to work with it. In other words, I get them to participate as much as possible so it is their session—not just me standing in front of them, talking to them.

Sandra Smith, learning and development manager for the Denver Public Library, sees herself both as a role model for the participants and as a leader for the organization: "I show up in a leader role for the organization and then layer on that as a role model for championing learning and sharing among my colleagues."

Maurice Coleman, technical trainer for the Harford County Public Library, sees himself as "a sherpa to get people from point A to the learning objectives. You help people get from where they are to the learning objectives. It's your job to use whatever tools you have to get people from where they are to where they need to be."

MANAGING AND FACILITATING CHANGE

During our interviews, we briefly explored whether there is a difference between managing change (in the sense of attempting to control it) and facilitating change (in the sense of proposing ways to engage in change without dictating a predetermined method for implementing that change)—a conceptual distinction that may be little more than semantic variation but may also imply a difference in intent on the part of those in charge of workplace learning and performance programs.

"I have been listening lately to a few online sessions dealing with facilitating groups," Catherine Vaughn says.

> I would like to implement some of the concepts I am learning from these sessions into my instructional course work because I feel it will

make for a more positive learning environment. Change management and change facilitation, I feel, have different meanings and ways of approaching the idea at hand. Management implies that you are there to tell them what they will do and how they will do it or get there, versus facilitation, where you will guide them through the process yet be there to keep everyone moving and offering ideas if the process gets stuck. . . . Facilitation implies that the participants will be taking a very active role in the process or learning environment. Facilitation creates the feeling that the work is from the participants, not management.

"I guess I like [the term] 'change facilitation' better because it's probably more accurate, but ultimately [it is] six of one, half dozen of the other," says Princeton Public Library assistant director Peter Bromberg. "I do tend to view myself as more a facilitator, which [is] about influence rather than management or control. I'm a big believer in influence. Control is an illusion, and one that causes a lot of pain. We're lucky if we can control ourselves—forget other people or circumstances! But we can always, always influence!"

Reading books on facilitation is a suggestion Bromberg makes to those new to workplace learning and performance: "I think the coaching books I've read—especially *Co-Active Coaching*[1]—have been very helpful, especially because many coaching books cover the effective use of listening and asking questions. . . . Effective facilitation is so much about that—listening deeply, reflecting back the essence of what it said, making connections with other ideas and comments, and using questions to engage students and get them thinking more deeply about the material and their relation to it."

"I see change management as a process," says Sandra Smith,

—big picture strategy for the organization or person or group . . . and change facilitation as an activity or collection of activities to foster/implement the change management. Process versus activity. The organization can't be successful in change management without understanding it as a process that needs structure, care, time, and directed activities to be successful—it is not a mandate from on high that is delivered and dropped on people.

Regarding my learning program: change is a foundational reality—excitement and, yes, challenge. As a learning manager, I must embrace—even more than just acknowledge—the reality of change in the work of my library and the work that I do. I look at its impact on every decision I make, short-term and long-term, and I push it out there for others to do the same as a leader in my library. If I am friends with it, then I respect it, learn from it, and use and leverage it to work for me and my goals.

For Pioneer Library System training coordinator Louise Whitaker,

the term "change management" implies that they will change whether they like it or not, because it is what the organization has decided. "Change facilitation" implies that change is going to happen for the organization to move forward, but it is done in a less structured manner. Perhaps it is a matter of taking a little longer period of time to make the change so staff will be better informed of the reasoning behind the change and they will have more buy-in.

GETTING TO KNOW YOU

Setting the stage is essential for any training/learning session. It is helpful to be familiar with the layout of the room in advance of the training to get a feel for the furniture arrangement, lighting, equipment, acoustics, and temperature.

An important part of the learning experience includes having a supportive and safe environment; if learners do not feel safe and have their basic needs—food, water, and comfort—met, they will be operating at a disadvantage when the time for learning arrives. Music is a great way to set the mood as participants arrive. Greeting and talking with participants as they enter the classroom or arrive for an online session provide an opportunity to establish rapport before the session formally begins.

Consultant Pat Wagner says she is surprised by the number of trainers who do not greet people as they come into the room: "I will take the handouts and stand at the back . . . or I will walk around and talk to people. . . . I'm responsible for the emotional state of the room. . . . I'm sometimes appalled by how many instructors will give the impression that they are distant and superior actors on a stage; the old Shakespearian actors would interact with their audience. Treating [learners] like a group of strangers just amazes me."

Wagner does what many of us have learned to do: engage in the personal one-on-one elements of establishing rapport by shaking hands, saying hello, and telling participants that we are glad to see them. If we are greeting learners online, equivalent actions can include sending one-on-one chat messages to people as they arrive and encouraging learning session participants to use live chat tools to converse with each other from the moment they arrive—a great way to create the sort of engagement Maurice Coleman and others use so effectively before, during, and even after learning opportunities to overcome the reticence and feeling of distance that many students have during their initial excursions into online learning.

"Show interest in the person as an individual," Sandra Smith agrees. "Meet them where they are—in both their skill level and attitude level."

Another benefit of taking this time to interact with our participants and become familiar with those we do not already know before a training session is that it gives us, as trainer-leader-facilitators, a chance to calm our own nerves; remember that Paul Witt's suggestion that fear of public speaking may be hard-wired into us (see chapter 4) does not offer an exemption for workplace learning and performance professionals. Even the most experienced public speakers can become nervous before speaking before a group, so finding ways to channel that nervous energy is helpful. Making these initial connections with participants helps us find those friendly faces in the audience during our presentation.

Elaine Biech, in *Training for Dummies,* writes that trainers should build interest in the session from the start. "Save the ground rules and the housekeeping details for later. Be creative with your opening. . . . Participants will want to know what's in it for them: how what they learn will be useful to them personally or how it will make their jobs easier."[2]

Wagner likes to set people up for success as quickly as possible.

> What if somebody sticks you in a class on conflict management? Maybe they're using words you've never heard before. You may feel a loss of self-esteem. Maybe you never graduated from high school. And here in front of you is someone with a master's or a PhD. Now they are saying what I consider the most deadly sentence in the world, "It's really easy," because you know that it probably isn't really easy for you. It may be really hard.
>
> So, I need to find a way to make people feel competent and confident quickly.

WHO'S RUNNING THE ASYLUM?

Nearly everyone interviewed for this book cited trainers reading verbatim from notes or PowerPoint slides as one of the worst mistakes we can make in workplace learning and performance. The key is to incorporate those slides into our presentations without repeating what they offer or letting them become a center of attention rather than a tool. In *Training for Dummies,* Elaine Biech is explicit about the difference between engaging in learning through interactions and serving as little more than a reader of material on slides or notes: "A trainer *is* a facilitator. Let me correct that. An *effective* trainer is a facilitator."[3]

In discussing the role of a facilitator, Pat Wagner says that,

> if you are using Socratic method and asking good questions, the role of someone like [a good trainer in] the room is we really do know more about certain aspects, but as much as we can, we want our students to come up with the answers themselves and for us to plug in the holes. . . . I ask a question, someone comes up with something, and I say, "That's great, and you know that in addition this works as well." That means that I become a collaborator. The danger is when you have trainers who practice the "trainer as smart cookie" model, which I can fall into. Too often, I'm a show-off. I want to be the star. I want to be the know-it-all. And that's how it comes off to participants.

Many of us admit that it is difficult to balance the showmanship that comes with being a trainer with giving up control and trusting that our participants will come up with the right responses to open-ended questions. One of us learned this mantra in a train-the-trainer session: "He who is doing the talking is doing the learning." This is the essence of the Socratic method of facilitation. Our adult learners bring with them vast amounts of knowledge and experience. Letting them share their wisdom with the group is what makes adult learning such a rewarding experience for us. Our colleagues confirm what we know: we learn as much during our sessions as the participants gain.

Jay Turner agrees and adds a bit of balance into the discussion of facilitation:

> If you're talking more than 60 percent of the time, you're talking too much. If your learners are talking over you, you're letting the inmates run the asylum. You balance the need for flexibility and structure versus total chaos by realizing from the outset that your job is not to script your training. If you're doing that, it begs the question, why even present live in the first place when you could just send your learners a verbatim transcript?
>
> The balance is found by truly understanding your role as a trainer: to facilitate learning in an environment where your students are equally important to the learning process as you the instructor. The instructor outlines the class content, is knowledgeable so that he can speak conversantly on the subject matter, and builds in learning activities to help learners retain the information. The instructor also must be flexible enough so that he isn't a slave to his outline.

"I use my facilitator skills to manage the chaos, e.g., managing the errant conversation, pulling it back to the framework, dealing with people's personalities," Sandra Smith notes. "I also use the mutual purpose theme from my *Crucial Conversations*[4] teaching—I rein in the chaos by reminding people why we are here and what our mission together is in the training time together. I keep an open communication with them on what I need to do for them and how they can best be a part of it."

In her sessions, Wagner has what she calls an "old school" approach to facilitating learning:

> I have handouts, outlines, cheat sheets, and worksheets so people can take notes and annotate the material while they are learning. I speak at most of the major, national library conferences—which are going paperless—and I will print out the handouts even when they are available online. As recently as the end of this year, I stood at the front of the room at a conference where the handouts were available online at least a week before the conference, and I asked participants if they wanted copies of the handouts. Maybe three had printed them out ahead of time and maybe ten had online versions on their laptops. Everyone else asked for a set.

Catherine Vaughn takes an entirely different approach: "I do not give copies of the PowerPoint slides. I find they are just filed away and not referred to later. I distribute worksheets for active participation in order for [participants] to apply what we have just discussed. I break people into groups a lot for discussion and thought-provoking ideas."

Vaughn also works to assure that the classroom does not degenerate into Turner's inmate-run asylum:

> This can be a difficult thing to do. If side conversations come up and they are not planned, I regroup by doing an "Okay, let's step back a minute and address the most recent comment that has so many of us buzzing about." This brings us back together without breaking the enthusiasm.
>
> If a conversation has led us totally in another direction, I will sometimes take a break to get everyone to stop talking about the misdirection, and, when we regroup, I pick up with the last topic I have in my notes, not what path we have gone down. Or if a break isn't doable, I will say something like, "Wow, you guys really have a lot of thoughts on this topic. Right now, I want you to write two words that

best describe what you are thinking [or] feeling about this topic and the direction it has taken. This will help you remember what other issues we will need to consider for topics for future classes." And then I direct back to my last comment for the class topic.

I like to find ways to let my adult learners feel in control of the experience, even if it is something as simple as letting them roll dice to figure out how long a restroom break will be or invite them to explore a topic related to my content that did not necessarily make it into my presentation. This can be good for working with people who have a need-to-know approach to learning.

"I don't see the trainer as needing to control the room," Peter Bromberg says:

I see the trainer's job as creating a structure—the lesson plan—and an environment for learning to take place. The trainer is then more a facilitator, knowing what the end goal is and moving things in the right direction. . . . Every class is going to be different because every class will have a unique group of people. Even if you're teaching the group week after week, they are having new experiences and having the normal ups [and] downs of daily life. So the idea that you can control the class is, to me, nonsensical. And more to the point, not an effective way to teach.

"Influence, not control," is the key to success, he says in summary.

IMPROVISATION, COMEDY, AND STAGE FRIGHT

Flexibility is important in face-to-face and online learning, Peter Bromberg reminds us:

It's important to be flexible, to listen and adjust the content and pace to what's happening with the class in that moment. More and more, I'm trying to design for less lecture and more experiential learning.

Asking good questions and showing patience [are] also very important—good questions being questions that challenge the learners to think about the material in relation to their experiences and beliefs, which helps them understand, integrate, and own the learning.

As for process, I spend a lot of time on the design. First, getting very clear about the goal of the training, and factoring in all the variables about the audience: who are they, what do they already know, what will the mood/motivation likely be? All of that is very, very important. Then I spend a lot of time creating the lesson plan, trying to minimize lecture and maximize interactive pieces as much as possible to keep everyone engaged. I try to use humor as much as I can. Some I build in, some I just let happen in the moment.

Bromberg's love of flexibility in delivering learning opportunities creates the possibility of on-the-spot changes; he actually designs extra interactive exercises that he does not expect to have time to use, then looks at workshops "as being modular" so he can add elements on the spur of the moment, as needed. "In short, have a plan, but always have some extra pieces you can swap in and out as needed. I'd also recommend investing the time to develop good questions, and use them early and often," he says. "Questions that get people to relate the material to their own experience. Questions that invite them to reflect, examine, and make meaning. Open-ended questions."

Sandra Smith says, "You know the expression 'if mama ain't happy, no one is happy'? Well, I'm mama in the classroom, and if I'm not having fun, then chances are no one is—and I use that fun for me to stay on and engaged, and it helps my energy stay high, which often leeches into the energy of attendees—so they tell me. And humor is really shown in studies to be an effective tool in adult learning engagement."

Jay Turner agrees:

> Improv is huge in delivering training live online or live in a classroom. My experience has been that it's not a day of training until something goes wrong. I find that I improv most during these situations, even when you've planned for worst-case scenarios. I like to keep a few activities and types of discussion ideas in the back of my mind that can be adapted for almost any situation. This way your learners will have something meaningful to do while you work on fixing the problem.
>
> The other time improv comes into play is when the flow of your class goes off track or on a major tangent. I've found great teachable moments in tangent discussions, and I'm sometimes hesitant to shut down the sidebar if something useful is coming from it. The drawback is that you're now unscripted and must rely on your trainer's instincts. . . . you can still keep structure to these tangents by relying on those canned discussion questions and activities, and then tie the tangent back into your presentation.

"I do find that it is helpful to be flexible," Catherine Vaughn says. "It allows the participants to think I am changing things because of them—they feel like they are a part of the learning process."

Keeping them engaged by not running a static session is also important for Maurice Coleman. One of the practices he and many of us use is to walk around the room rather than conduct an entire session from one stationary spot. "People will watch you and pay attention," Coleman confirms. "If you have a small class of people talking, this is an easy way to stop this. Present from where they are. Make sure people are awake. . . . In computer labs you can't see anything other than heads" unless you walk around.

Turner also speaks passionately of the importance of paying attention to learners "to be sure they are attentive. I watch for facial expressions and body language in a face-to-face setting. I use the attention-monitoring function of WebEx when presenting live, online training."

Like others, Coleman focuses strongly on maintaining connections with his learners rather than give too much attention to the tools he uses. With this in mind, he strongly objects to reading directly from PowerPoint slides: "Please do not read your blasted slides. You are wasting everyone's time. You could have just handed them out." He also follows a pattern many of us incorporate into our work: using humor in all he does—including answering interview questions for this book. "I consider myself a very bad amateur comedian, so I use it a lot," he quips. "Humor can break the ice, so it's part of your toolkit. It can lighten the mood [and] you can tell if people are listening to you."

"Humor provides positive energy," Pat Wagner agrees. "A good hearty laugh can get people's energy up for 45 minutes and substitute for a cup of coffee or a soft drink. Laughter also helps alleviate fear or anxiety about learning. . . . If I get everybody laughing, it's like giving everybody an injection of fearlessness so they don't get glued into a position."

"The trick, of course, with humor" Turner warns, "is that you have to be sensitive to your audience. What might be funny to you could be caustic to someone else. My advice is to keep it clean and corny, and you'll be fine."

A final point Coleman makes is to "stretch your boundaries [and] take risks, if you are able to." "Use failure as a learning tool" rather than miss that learning opportunity by always following a safe and predictable route in the training-teaching-learning process, he concludes.

Taking risks is part of leadership, Wagner says:

> My personal definition of leadership includes risk, vision, influence, and character. . . . When I think of the things we just talked about, I think about the fact that, as a leader, I have to be willing to take risks. For example, in the last eight months, I was using a particular technology tool to conduct training. In the middle of a six-week class, the technology broke, so I said to the class, "I really screwed up, I picked

the wrong technology" . . . and I apologized. One of the students said, "You really modeled leadership." The fact is that you're going to screw up sometimes, and you have to be good enough to tell your class, "I screwed up."

The vision part is to keep our eyes on the sky. We're doing training; it's not just for personal enrichment. We're being paid in the workplace.

The influence part is the conscious ability to inspire. The best compliment I've ever had was from the librarian who told me that my class helped her feel braver. With character, I think I have an obligation to be a better person. . . . In a classroom, I have to be a better person than who I really am.

Each of us has our own list of items we try to avoid while working with learners, and Smith's seems to include nearly all of them: "not being prepared; whining about something about the organization, the room, the technology, or having to do the training; not showing inclusiveness to all the attendees; letting someone sidetrack the class; not taking time to arrange, when possible, the classroom in a way that is conducive to learning."

An additional tip, offered by Louise Whitaker, is "never to put someone down, or make them feel stupid. While we all know not to do this in an obvious manner, it is important to be aware of our audience so we don't say or do something unintentionally to belittle them. Another to be careful of is calling someone out by name to answer a question. Some people would rather be beaten than speak in public, and we have to respect that while trying to keep them engaged."

"Impatience on the part of the trainer is one of the biggest problems," she adds.

With those reminders, we are almost where we need to be.

MAKING IT STICK

Trainers as leaders know that it is not enough to complete a lesson plan, collect favorable evaluations, and pretend that success has been achieved. What happens after learners leave a session is the critically important element in all that we do, so we build activities into the learning process to promote the use of what is learned rather than hand out a certificate of completion and go home.

"I try a few things in the classroom or online to ensure learning—at least some—is taking place," notes Catherine Vaughn.

I ask them to apply what we were discussing to an exercise that I am now handing out. I ask them to tell me how they can use or implement what we have just discussed—give me a situation when this idea/ concept could have been helpful. . . . If the session is online, I have them complete a questionnaire that covers the topics we discussed but does not directly answer the question; I expect them to use their processing skills to come up with the correct answer.

"I usually build some form of follow-up into learning," Jay Turner says. "This can be a formal assignment or simply e-mailing participants afterward and letting them know that I'm available to answer lingering questions by phone, e-mail, or meeting one-on-one online through WebEx."

Maurice Coleman uses an even more basic approach to make learning stick: "Encourage curiosity. That is the most important thing in my twenty years as a trainer. Allow people the space to not feel stupid asking a question. . . . The deeper meaning is that you want to have your adult learners take some responsibility— through humor. The bottom line is that you and I are both responsible for your learning. Be proactive. If you do not understand, ask."

After encouraging them to ask, the next step in the learning process is to determine what our learners have done with the answers, as we see in chapter 6. In the meantime, as Pat Wagner suggests, trainers should engage in what Robert Greenleaf calls "servant leadership."[5] "The highest level of my success is that the person in front of me becomes that leader . . . and doesn't need me anymore," she explains.

> When you focus on that idea, it's as if you've got your hands like a stirrup under someone's foot and you're about to propel them on a trajectory toward what they are trying to reach. . . . If you choose the role of being a servant first . . . you don't want to be the star in the room; you want to be the leader. It goes back to the idea that the ultimate goal of service organizations is to put ourselves out of business because we are not needed anymore. I see too many situations where there is competition between the student and the instructor.

NOTES

1. Laura Whitworth, Henry Kimsey-House, and Phil Sandhahl, *Co-Active Coaching: New Skills for Coaching People toward Success in Work and Life* (Mountain View, Calif.: Davies-Black, 2007).
2. Elaine Biech, *Training for Dummies* (Hoboken: Wiley, 2005), 159
3. Ibid., 138.
4. Kerry Patterson, Joseph Grenny, Ron McMillan, and Al Switzler, *Crucial Conversations: Tools for Talking When Stakes Are High* (New York: McGraw-Hill, 2002).
5. Robert Greenleaf, *Servant Leadership: A Journey into the Nature of Legitimate Power and Greatness* (New York: Paulist Press, 1977).

6

WHEN LEARNING HAPPENS
SUPPORTING LEARNERS AFTER CLASS

I think the person who plays the largest role is the supervisor
in the follow-up arena.

—Catherine Vaughn, Continuing Education Coordinator,
Lee County Library System

Talk to most learners in the days after they return from a face-to-face or
online session, and you will hear what we call the Learner's Lament: "I
wish I had time to use what I learned." This, of course, raises a question
for all of us: what are we doing here? "Too many times, a person comes back to
their place of work and is never asked to discuss, demonstrate, implement . . .
what learning took place in a session. If learning is not reinforced soon, much
is quickly lost," Lee County Library System continuing education coordinator
Catherine Vaughn says, capturing the heart of the challenges we address in
this chapter. We have already discussed the dirty little secret that really is not
a secret among those involved in library and nonprofit workplace learning and
performance programs: most training does not lead to changes in the workplace.
It is, to be blunt, time wasted.

As we look specifically at what happens in the hours, days, weeks, and months
after someone completes a lesson and returns to the workplace, we realize we are
about to face a critically important issue. If we, as leaders in workplace learning and performance, do not create an environment that supports the changes
encouraged through the lessons we are offering, we might as well not waste our
time, our colleagues' time, and our organizations' time.

Now that we have bluntly and harshly described the challenge we all face, let's consider what we and others are and can be doing to reverse this situation. Providing effective learning opportunities is, after all, far from being an insurmountable challenge; we have all had those moments of success and celebration when we learned to do something we needed to learn to do. What we need to accomplish with greater regularity is moving past the idea that training is what happens while the student is with us and embrace a larger and far more positive belief that training is an ongoing process drawing from the creation of communities of learning. Workplace learning and performance initiatives are most successful when everyone involved displays a commitment to use what is learned in the broadest possible terms to the benefit of all we serve.

A MODIFIED MODEL FOR SUCCESS

We have already, in a brief way in chapter 4, reviewed one of the linchpins of training-teaching-learning: the ADDIE model and its slightly updated sibling, ARDDIE. As we focus on what happens between the time a learner completes a lesson and the time when we complete and review the results of formal evaluations, we realize there is yet another missing link that many of our learners readily and ruefully acknowledge: follow-up designed to help learners absorb and apply what they have learned. It is not our intention to add to the already jargon-laden world of training, so we are not going to suggest an ARDDIFE model—mainly because we have no idea how we would even begin pronouncing that newly coined acronym—but we are going to acknowledge that printed sources and training colleagues we are citing throughout this book agree that follow-up is every bit as important to the learning process as the other steps are.

Evaluation being the important and often undervalued element of workplace learning and performance that it is, it is the entire focus of the next chapter; for now, we explore what happens between completion of a formal learning opportunity and implementation of an effective evaluation process.

Management consultant and trainer Pat Wagner is someone who displays an instinctive sense of the importance of making learning a process rather than taking a day-of-the-event approach. Even while engaged in the presentation of material to learners, she thinks ahead:

> My closing exercise is to ask people how they are going to apply the information from the class or, if they were teaching a class on this topic, what would they include from the material I presented. Or, even

if it's not something directly related to the class . . . "what do you think you're going to apply when you return to your workplace?"

Anything I can do to get them to reflect on the material and then come back with something that is about how they will apply it—it can't be about my success, it can't be about the Pat Wagner Fan Club. Whatever happens outside of the classroom, if it inspires change, it is a success.

"Overall, I want to find out if the experience was a productive and rewarding one for both attendees and instructors," Denver Public Library learning and development manager Sandra Smith agrees. "I . . . regularly speak with staff, both informally in following up with individuals about their experiences and needs and informally on-the-fly in hallways, around meetings, in the parking lots, etc., to get reactions . . . to what's being offered."

"When it comes to my leadership role in providing follow-up to training, I'm more of a coordinator," Gwinnett County Public Library training manager Jay Turner observes of his own approach.

I may send follow-up activities [for] my learners to complete within a given timeframe after class, and then the responsibility is often placed on that staff member's supervisor to ensure that the follow-up is completed. . . . Likewise, I may send a behavioral checklist to a trainee's supervisor so that the supervisor can observe for performance changes. Also, depending on the training initiative, I may send follow-up assessments to staff and supervisors to see if the learning is being used in the work environment.

Taking that level of interest in and sustaining that level of involvement in follow-up efforts is not easy, Catherine Vaughn admits: "Follow-up is sometimes a difficult task to manage. I feel the trainer-facilitator can play a role. However, I think the person who plays the largest role is the supervisor in the follow-up arena." It is with this comment that we find ourselves directly in the middle of what is missing from so many learning opportunities: the personal involvement and support of key players and stakeholders, and a personal and organizational commitment to creating the sort of workplace where, when learners return from formal lessons, they are encouraged to implement what they have learned.

Let's not forget that this is neither academic nor theoretical: it is about people, performance, and results. Even though we all appreciate and acknowledge how difficult it is for us as individuals to find or make the time to engage in this level of support, we should be puzzled and even somewhat disappointed in ourselves that we acquiesce in letting those limitations of time and resources stop us, since so much has been written about the importance of follow-up and workplace support. We must instinctively know—even if we have not seen the research available to us—that what we are doing could be much more effective than it is, but we do not seem to have reached the point where we feel compelled to invest the time and effort it requires to be strong advocates for the improvements our minds and hearts are nudging us to pursue. We are not even encouraged by those in positions above us to follow up continually with our learners and make sure that a transfer of learning has taken place from the learning space to the workplace. Instead, we are rushed from one training assignment to the next without the time to complete effectively the assignment we are pursuing.

James Kouzes and Barry Posner provide great guidance and inspiration for us as we consider what we might be doing better as learning leaders; they effectively document throughout their book *The Leadership Challenge* the obvious and important influences leaders have on those around them. Their "Five Practices and Ten Commitments of Leadership" include reminders that leaders "model the way," "inspire a shared vision," "challenge the process," "enable others to act," and "encourage the heart," and their suggested commitments include one to "set the example by aligning actions with shared values"—ideas that we all too often set aside as we deal with the varied and conflicting directives coming our way.[1]

Furthermore, citing their extensive research, Kouzes and Posner remind us of the tremendous influence leaders—we—have: "If you're a manager in an organization, to *your* direct reports *you* are the *most important* leader in your organization. . . . The leaders who have the most influence on people are those who are the *closest* to them," they write. "You have to challenge the myth that leadership is about position and power."[2]

There is no reason to believe that such influential leadership would not carry over into the realm of influencing and supporting learners, and there is every reason to believe we might achieve better results for our learners, our organizations, and all whom we ultimately serve if we managed somehow to push a few other challenges aside long enough to take advantage of the possibilities offered by the positions we hold or hope to hold. After all, if we and those around us do not feel it is important enough to model what we offer and to support its implementation, we can hardly be surprised by the awful and frankly embarrassing news that what is learned is generally implemented by approximately 15 percent of those attending training sessions.[3]

Because this number is so staggering, we should stop for a moment to reflect upon it. If only 15 percent of what is learned transfers back to the job, what happens to the other 85 percent? Does it float out the window as the learner daydreams during class? Does it pass into the realms of social networking as learners update their Twitter and Facebook statuses during class, or are we teaching ideals that are simply not possible in the real world of today's libraries and nonprofit organizations, which are constantly under threat of closure or are facing imminent reductions in funding?

If we dive one level deeper and return to the idea that training is all about change, we find encouragement in Everett Rogers's *Diffusion of Innovation* as we contemplate the influence we might have within the change-facilitation aspects of the learning process, and much of this comes within the follow-up phase we are promoting in this chapter. "Opinion leaders" and "change agents," Rogers maintains, are critical in providing a setting in which change can occur. As Kouzes and Posner maintain and Rogers tells us, "Informal leadership is not a function of the individual's formal position or status in the system. Opinion leadership is earned and maintained by the individual's technical competence, social accessibility, and conformity to the system's norms."[4]

"Innovation champions"—those who actually champion the innovation being suggested in any context, including library and nonprofit organization's workplace learning and performance efforts—furthermore, "can play an important role in boosting a new idea in an organization. . . . Past research shows that an innovation champion is often important in the innovation process in organizations," Rogers maintains.[5]

One such example of an innovation champion is Helene Blowers, former technology director for the Charlotte Mecklenburg Library. Blowers saw that classroom training was not getting enough staff up to speed fast enough with Web 2.0 technology, so she created a list of "23 Things" that all staff needed to know about Web 2.0 (see chapter 2). Lists of competencies are nothing new, but the stroke of brilliance with the Learning 2.0/23 Things program was the follow-through conducted to ensure that participants understood what they were learning.

As participants learned each thing, they were required to write blog posts summarizing the lesson. Many participants, however, went above and beyond what was required by not only summarizing what they learned but also actually performing the lesson in the blog posts. In "thing five," for example, participants were assigned to "explore Flickr and learn about this popular image hosting site." Many participants created Flickr accounts, uploaded photos, and then embedded those photos in their blog posts. This was the transfer of learning that trainers crave.

It is no wonder that this program has been replicated by libraries around the world. Michael Stephens, assistant professor in the Graduate School of Library and Information Science at Dominican University in Illinois, has been conducting research in Australia to understand the impact on library staff and institutional culture and makeup after a Learning 2.0 program. In a survey given to Australian library workers who had completed the Learning 2.0 program, 89 percent of the 318 respondents said they were now confident or very confident in learning new technologies.[6]

In a 2007 article in *Computers in Libraries,* Blowers herself reflected on the intangible benefits the program provided to her staff: "In the end, the program not only created a bond among workers at individual branches but also helped to strengthen our staff community systemwide."[7]

From a trainer's point of view, what makes the 23 Things program work is that it takes training out of the classroom and puts learning front and center in the hands of the learners. The trainer is there to create the exercises and to guide and encourage staff along the way, but the responsibility for learning is ultimately in the hands of the learner—where it should be. This self-directed approach to learning rather than training allows the learner to apply immediately what is learned in relation to the learner's job or personal interests. This immediacy and this choice of how to apply what is being learned are what makes the learning stick.

It is clear, as we resurface from this brief exploration of a few well-respected and well-established models, that we have our work cut out for us. If we move directly from delivery of learning opportunities to the evaluation of the results produced by those learning opportunities—or, even worse, if we focus on the moment of delivery as the entire learning process rather than see the moment of delivery as part of a much more important, long-range, and potentially effective process that benefits all stakeholders—we miss a critically important phase of the process—the follow-up that leads to positive change. The result, of course, will be the continuing and pathetic 15 percent success rate mentioned by Brinkerhoff and others.

"I do believe that the ultimate measure of success [in training] is success in behavior after time in the classroom," Wagner says. "I don't work in an institution and I don't supervise, so the best I can do is to be sure that every supervisor is a trainer. . . . It is in that supervisory role that . . . change is dispersed throughout the organization."

Wagner also offers support for the idea that there must be an alignment between what is offered through learning sessions and what is supported in the learner's workplace: "If I am the staff member attending the program, before I even go to class I [need to] have that conversation with my supervisor about the class and, after the class, I have a debriefing [about what is usable and what will be applied]. That kind of planning is very important."

"That should happen most of the time if the supervisor is doing her job before and after the class"—but it rarely does, Wagner adds:

> I would say [it happens] five to ten percent of the time. Mostly what I see and hear from the training staff of libraries—and I believe what they are saying is legitimate—[is that] someone in the institution says, "Train everybody in whatever," and people are not given enough time and not given enough information. There's no institutional follow-up, and there are no positive or negative consequences, so if I go to a class and study real hard . . . when I come back, nobody says anything about the class. If I apply the materials, nobody says anything. If I don't apply the materials, nobody says anything. That's where I become apathetic. . . . There's a dual message I hear: "You go to training, but we really don't care."

Wagner has described a fundamental breakdown between management and training. If library and nonprofit leaders refuse to put methods in place to hold employees accountable for not only knowing what was presented in training but also for applying those lessons back on the job, then once again we must ask ourselves, what is it that we are really doing here?

As trainers become leaders within their own organizations, they must find ways to educate members of administration and management about the important role they play in training. Without strong support from those key players, training is a waste of time. The employees know it. Often the trainer is the last to admit or realize this grim reality. No one wants to be set up to fail.

WHAT OUR COLLEAGUES SAY AND DO

Sandra Smith, with her Denver Public Library colleagues, takes the most comprehensive day-to-day approach we encountered among our colleagues in terms of supporting change through learning after formal lessons have been completed:

> I . . . do a post-wrap with any stakeholders—executive team, managers—to inform them of what has happened . . . to both keep them informed and to let them know of reactions, further needs, failures, and anything else they need to know for immediate and strategic purposes. For our larger initiatives, I do create reports showing aggregate info from evaluations—I always make sure that I have some quantifiable data, as

well as open responses—so this data can be a part of our measurable and ROI organizational needs.

I do not do this for every simple info session [there are more than 150 each year at Denver Public] but do for the "biggies" that have been specifically targeted. I also track data about who attends each class, their positions, etc., so I can at any time pull up info on the demographics of our learning program and I use this in an annual report.

As is often the case with those who seem to be most innovative and far-reaching in setting expectations for themselves, Smith adds a caveat: "I need to do more with individual learners' post-sessions, and that is a priority for me in the coming year."

We have already made it clear in this chapter that we believe we need to shift our priorities a bit to take into account the need for more follow-up. We should be equally explicit that this does not simply mean taking on even more responsibilities and hastening the inevitable moment of burnout that causes great organizations to lose equally great employees; we need to find a way to remove some of the dross that comes our way and focus on, as well as advocate, the sort of balanced workload and job description that allow us to produce the results our colleagues deserve.

When someone higher up in our organizational hierarchy tells us that we are being assigned to yet another committee or project that has nothing to do with our workplace learning and performance responsibilities, we need to make a case—diplomatically and convincingly—for returning to the overall priorities the organization has set for its training programs. There is no use pretending that any organization can thrive in a setting where no good deed goes unpunished or every goal successfully reached is immediately rewarded with two new tasks to complete. We are, after all, trainer-teacher-learners at heart; we rely on a well-developed knowledge of educational techniques, highly refined communication and facilitation skills, and an aptitude for effectively creating communities of learning. If we remind ourselves that we have and can employ these skills and do all we can to advocate effective use of those skills, we will sleep better at night, and our colleagues will gain more from us than if we allow ourselves to be pulled in so many directions that we accomplish bits and pieces of everything without fully achieving anything substantial.

Still, in the new reality many organizations are facing, trainers in fear of job cuts are taking on other roles to avoid being affected by layoffs. Many trainers serve dual roles simply because of their place on an organizational chart. Trainers who work in a human resources department often take on other human resource tasks. Likewise, trainers who work in information technology departments take on help desk responsibilities. The worst situation is faced within organizations that do not have the funding to support a full-time staff development position. Training within libraries and nonprofit organizations facing those situations is piecemeal and often offered by staff members torn between their customer service, staff development, and other responsibilities.

"Ideally, I would be more involved in the transfer of training process, but I'm a department of one. My reality is that I spend a significant portion of my time dealing with the daily minutiae of managing the training function. I have an LMS to oversee, a budget to run, papers to push, and fires to extinguish," Jay Turner readily admits in words that almost everyone we know who is involved in library and nonprofit workplace learning and performance programs could repeat.

Smith offers a reminder that we cannot hear enough: "My job as a leader is to see that the scale remains overall in balance." "We, as learning leaders, need to have high expectations for what we want our staff and organization to look like and then take those expectations and match them with the realities of organizational resources, culture, needs, and human capacity and capability," she quickly adds. "It may look one way for my library and another way for someone else, but as long as we each are honestly and with our best integrity and skills striving to a high expectation, it is enough and should be celebrated."

Her comment about celebration offers us even more food for thought in terms of what we can do to implement effective follow-up: remember to celebrate large and small achievements—something we build into the learning process only infrequently.

One of us, in working with a group of learners who were facing large challenges in adapting to a new technology their organization was introducing, could see that the learners not only were drained at the end of each session but were walking away a bit discouraged. It was clear that they were learning what they needed to learn, and it was equally clear that they were too immersed in the process to recognize how much they were achieving—all they could see was what they still needed to learn, not what they had already learned. Those of us working on that particular learning project, during one of our end-of-the-day reviews of how the lessons had gone, noted that we needed to do something to reduce the learners' overall stress level and inject a bit of levity into the process, so we decided to introduce an upbeat "victory dance" video from YouTube into the next day's lesson.

When the learners returned the following day for what everyone knew was going to be the longest and most intense of the formal lessons, we outlined our lesson plan and referred obliquely to the victory dance we would do at the end of class. It was obvious from the learners' body language and smiles that they knew the course was about to take a shift in tone, so we suspected we were onto something positive. As promised, when the lesson ended and the learners had demonstrated their mastery of the material covered, we projected the brief video onto a blank wall in the front of the classroom, and though no one actually stood up and emulated the victory dance we had discovered, they all left the classroom smiling. The real payoff came at the end of the lesson on the following day: a few of the learners looked at those of us leading the latest session and asked, "Don't we get to see the dance again?"

Surprised and pleased that what we had done produced the desired effect—and, by the way, helped strengthen the sense that a community of learners was continuing to develop among the participants—we brought the video back up for those who wanted to watch it again. Having learned our own lesson from that experience, we then built celebratory, humorous video vignettes into each subsequent module of the course, and we continue to remember and promote the idea that the little effort it takes to build celebration into the learning process produces results far beyond what any of us might expect.

Returning for one final pass over the theme of what our colleagues offer as best practices, we once again find Smith offering great hands-on, practical guidance:

> I encourage staff teachers to follow up with reminders...[and] questions to people about what's happening with them around their daily work and the training. I also make sure that an atmosphere of "call on me anytime" is put out there by staff teachers and myself—cultivating an open communication process. . . . Teachers are encouraged to check in, and we just now have on our Intranet Learning Pages, an online forum where all staff can contribute their thoughts about anything in the learning arena—comments, sharables, questions, suggestions. These come directly to me . . . and everyone who looks at them on the Learning Pages.

The Charlotte Mecklenburg Library has a similar model—Learning Discussion Forums—on its intranet. Employees are encouraged to post to discussion boards created for each course and to use those boards as a follow-up after training. For online training—both synchronous and asynchronous—posting to the discussion forums is not only required but built into the online lesson modules. At the beginning of any self-paced course, a link is posted to the discussion board and learners are encouraged to post questions there about the content of a course. Near the end of a course, learners are instructed to post a reflection of what they learned.

Catherine Vaughn also takes a supportive approach through the leaders within her organization:

> I encourage managers . . . [and] supervisors to follow up. This not only helps the supervisor get an idea if anything was retained, it also allows them to make the employee feel important. An employee can be the center of attention if sought out to get their opinion, ideas, etc. about the recently attended session. The employee may also feel, "Wow, he . . . [or] she does care. They [members of management] want me to do well."
>
> I do get to travel to most of our locations a few times throughout the year. When I am at a particular location, I try to follow up face-to-face with some of my participants. This shows that I remember that they attended, and it gives them a chance to tell me what they are using from the session. It also gives me great feedback about what got through and what didn't.

The Charlotte Mecklenburg Library is among those sending all of its managers and supervisors through courses before the sessions are open to frontline staff. This ensures that the leaders in the organization know what the employees will be learning and makes it easier for managers to follow up with their employees.

Turner's current practices include additional complementary elements: "I consistently invite learners to reach out to me with questions . . . if they want to further explore the subject. I'm also a proponent of teaching only need-to-know info, but I invite further exploration for my learners by including supplemental resources to explore." "Finally—and particularly with new employees—I'll sometimes contact my trainees, see how what was taught is jelling with the reality of their work environment, and then do something [to further support what has been learned]"—a comment that makes us want to be learners in any organization where those doing the hiring have been smart enough to hire Jay and turn him loose with learners.

When we turn to the question of what we wish we could be doing, Turner offers an ideal that many of us might envy:

> I would first evaluate the learning experience for the trainees and assess whether learning occurred. From there, I would send the learners back into their job environment but would include a place—likely online—where they could go and continue conversations relating to class. About a month out, after the training halo has worn off, I'd follow up with the learners and see what, if [any], skills learned/reinforced

from training are being used in the workplace. I would also ask their supervisors the same and compare those forms of feedback.

The Charlotte Mecklenburg Library has a goal to follow up training with Level 3 or 4 evaluations about a month after each course—a topic we examine in chapter 7.

WHAT OUR COLLEAGUES AVOID IN LEARNING AND IN FOLLOW-UP

Just as there are numerous things we can and should be doing to lay the groundwork for successful learning through follow-up, there are things we need to remind ourselves to not do with or to our learners. "Whining about what's taken place is a no-no in my book, especially doing it with people who you want to ultimately respect your efforts—and you theirs," Sandra Smith says. "Don't criticize the sincere efforts of those who are working with you in learning events. You'll taint the waters and never get back your credibility as a resource or leader." "Yes," she adds, "I indulge in occasional whining—but with folks I'm not serving as a role model!"

One of our mentors refers to this habit of whining or gossiping as "rolling in the mud" and frequently says, "You can't expect to remain clean if you are constantly rolling in the mud with other employees." As trainer-teacher-learners, we often have a unique connection with those we serve. We have interacted with nearly every employee in our organizations, and in many cases we have heard thoughts shared in the private setting of a classroom. Though it is easy to become comfortable and at ease with our coworkers, we need to remember that these same colleagues have also trusted us with their thoughts. This level of professionalism and ethical behavior is one of the attributes that set a great trainer-as-leader apart from a good trainer-as-leader.

TIPS AND ADMISSIONS

One of the practices we most admire in our colleagues is how much they take us back to basics: Pioneer Library System training coordinator Louise Whitaker, for example, tries to return to learners to see what they have retained: "In four months we follow up to see if they are using the information from the training, and if not, why? Was it not clear, or was it not directly job related?"

She also engages in follow-up at an even more basic level:

> I make a note of any questions that weren't answered and follow up
> to answer those, call them by name when I see them so they know I
> recognize them as an individual, and I keep in touch with supervisors
> so they feel free to call about [their] needs. I think all of our supervisors
> feel comfortable contacting me about training needs, whether it is
> something new or something that was just conducted. I often travel
> to our branches and conduct trainings for just the staff at that branch,
> which makes it more personal, and they feel freer to ask questions.
> . . . I think the new follow-ups we are implementing will be helpful, but
> I really wish we could conduct a secret shopper campaign to see the
> level of service from the customer perspective.

Jay Turner, in attempting to be effective in providing learning opportunities that stick, does not place himself above his learners, nor does he focus on learners' responsibilities to the exclusion of a trainer's critically important role: "A trainer should have a good feel for his or her learners before engaging in follow-up," he reminds us. "I know that we often have prepared follow-up activities built into our training outlines, but sometimes the learners you've worked with don't necessarily need your canned follow-up." "Be flexible," he adds.

Turner recalls a time when he was preparing to offer a webinar and, after working with the learners for nearly two weeks, decided to change the format of what he was preparing completely:

> I kept the webinar scheduled as planned, but instead of forcing them to
> attend and visit information that they probably had already mastered,
> I e-mailed my scripted PowerPoint presentation to them, told them
> to read it, and then dropped into the WebEx session I had originally
> scheduled to teach the class. If they had questions or wanted to discuss
> [the topic being taught], then I'd be there in WebEx for two hours
> willing to work . . . [or] discuss concepts with them one-on-one. Half
> the class popped in at various times to have the one-on-one time. In
> essence, empowering the new hires to review the PowerPoint at their
> leisure was the class, and the WebEx session was the follow-up—a
> flexible form of follow-up.

As facile as Turner is at facilitating both online and face-to-face learning, he agrees that follow-up presents a challenge. So does Sandra Smith: "I do want to say that this [follow-up] is the area that I and others know we need to work on more purposefully. It is, I think, a harder part of our jobs, as it's the more analytical piece, and most of us trainers love the 'people' piece most and get our internal rewards from that most often. But the follow-up is critical for both the success and survival of anyone's learning program."

NOTES

1. James Kouzes and Barry Posner, *The Leadership Challenge*, 4th ed. (San Francisco: John Wiley and Sons, 2007), 26.
2. Ibid., 338.
3. Robert O. Brinkerhoff, *Telling Training's Story: Evaluation Made Simple, Credible, and Effective* (San Francisco: Berrett-Koehler, 2006), 40.
4. Everett Rogers, *Diffusion of Innovation*, 5th ed. (New York: Free Press, 2003), 27.
5. Ibid., 414.
6. Michael Stephens and Warren Cheetham, "The Impact of Learning 2.0 Programs in Australian Libraries," http://research.tametheweb.com; Michael Stephens, "PLA Learning 2.0 Presentation," www.slideshare.net/mstephens7/pla-learning-20-presentation.
7. Helene Blowers and Lori Reed, "The C's of Our Sea Change: Plans for Training Staff, from Core Competencies to LEARNING 2.0," *Computers in Libraries*, February 2007: 10–15.

7

LEARNING FROM SUCCESS AND FAILURE
THE IMPORTANCE OF EFFECTIVE EVALUATIONS

You can't continue to go blindly into the future without having some sense of whether your previous workshops were successful or not.

—Rachel Vacek, Web Services Coordinator,
University of Houston Libraries

Documenting our successes (and our failures) by engaging in program evaluation can be like going to the dentist: almost all of us believe it is something we should do, and many of us keep it on our perpetual list of things to do—tomorrow. Talking with colleagues who are leaders in library and nonprofit workplace learning and performance programs shows that a few are quite advanced in how they approach the topic; those wonderful outliers who are far ahead of the rest of us routinely draw from some of the best resources, including Kirkpatrick's four levels of evaluation, and still say they wish they were doing even more.[1] Many others follow the more common path of having learners respond to a series of questions about whether they felt the instructor was effective, whether the training facilities or online coursework were conducive to learning, and whether they believe what they learned can be applied in their own workplace—without ever taking the time to see whether what was learned actually was used to the benefit of the learners and the organizations and customers they serve. A few others just keep thinking about tomorrow.

The consequences of ignoring our leadership roles in conducting evaluations or failing in any way to document successes often come when budgets are tight and libraries, nonprofits, and corporations are looking to cut costs in any way they can; those who cannot prove the benefits that workplace learning programs provide soon find their training budgets being slashed or completely eviscerated. The unfortunate irony, of course, is that training is often what is needed to help these organizations "do more with less," effectively do less with less, and help build the skills of existing staff. We are, therefore, going to spend considerable time in this chapter reviewing what we have read and what we have heard from colleagues involved in training programs. We also are sharing stories that offer a wide variety of reactions to the question of whether evaluations are providing worthwhile results to trainer-teacher-learners and all they serve.

KIRKPATRICK'S LEVELS OF EVALUATION

A first-rate starting point for any discussion about evaluation is the work of those who have preceded us; there is, after all, no reason any of us needs to re-create what already is in place. One writer often quoted in corporate training programs but not so recognizable among library and small-to-midlevel nonprofit organizations is Donald L. Kirkpatrick. Spend any time reading ASTD publications including the monthly *T+D* magazine or nearly any other in-depth examination of what contributes to a well-run learning program, and you will not go far before coming across references to his work—and for good reason. Kirkpatrick surmises that there are four levels through which we can evaluate the effectiveness of learning: reaction, learning, behavior, and results. What he looks for—and recommends we look for—are levels of change, since training and learning opportunities are generated to facilitate change among individuals and within organizations.

Kirkpatrick's Level 1 evaluation is the level most familiar to those of us engaged in evaluating and documenting the results of what we provide. It measures how the audience reacts to the training. Commonly called "smile sheets" because they are designed to tell us whether learners are smiling when they complete the lessons we provide, Level 1 evaluations tell little about whether any learning actually took place. Instead, the participants' initial reactions to the training are evaluated through questions that ask whether the participants are happy with the workshop, whether they believe the handouts are useful, and whether the room or method of online delivery is comfortable.

With Level 2, we begin to look for tangible effects by measuring what knowledge, skills, or attitudes are improved as a result of the learning that occurs. This can be measured through quizzes, more formal tests, or surveys administered before and after a learning opportunity has been completed. Although a Level 2 evaluation can prove that learning has occurred, it does not confirm that the learning will be applied back on the job, so Kirkpatrick takes us to a third level, where we look for behavioral changes in the workplace during the weeks and months following completion of a learning opportunity. If, for example, a learner completes a customer service course, we might look for proof that the learner has effectively demonstrated an ability to de-escalate an interaction with a hostile customer. If a learner has completed a workshop or course on a new piece of software, we look for proof that the software is being used more efficiently or effectively to the benefit of the individual, the organization, and those served by the organization.

In a Level 4 evaluation, we reach the pinnacle of showing why workplace learning and performance efforts are worth far more than anyone will ever invest in them. We attempt, at this stage, to show long-term results to the organization and those it serves. If, for example, we have offered that customer service course, we might seek evidence that circulation of the library's materials or use of its online resources has increased because of improved levels of service provided by the learner. We try to establish, through surveys or focus groups or other evaluation methods, that there has been an increase in the way a library's or nonprofit organization's customers express their satisfaction with the service they are receiving compared to how they rated customer service before the training occurred. We look for evidence that training provides other measurable, long-term benefits.

Most important, we work to develop a meaningful way to attach a dollar value or other quantifiable benefit that shows that the effort and expenditures produced worthwhile results. We might, for example, document that worker's compensation costs have decreased after employees completed health and safety or ergonomic training, or that the costs of litigating sexual harassment charges have dropped significantly because harassment-prevention training reduced the problem in the workplace. Because this is often the most difficult level to evaluate and document within libraries and nonprofit organizations, few of our colleagues tell us that they routinely engage in this effort. That does not, however, mean that it is not worth pursuing. If we do not ask, what chance do we, ourselves, have of learning?

BREAKTHROUGH TRAINING AND RESULTS

Because training is about change and obviously should document results, we are strong advocates of looking beyond facts and figures so we can see how our work ultimately affects those it is meant to serve. As we try to determine how our work affects learners, their organizations, and their customers, we start—rather than end—with simple results, including documenting how many people were served. The more important part of the process is to ask what ultimately happens to the learners and their customers as a result of the knowledge they acquired. We need to document how many of our colleagues actually attempted to use what they learned when they returned to their worksite, and then find ways to track how that learning experience filtered through our organizations to begin seeking, documenting, and learning from the more sustainable results a successful workplace learning and performance program produces.

We might, for example, ask whether a customer service training workshop led to better service to the customers themselves: As a result of receiving improved service, were they able to make some sort of measurable and positive change in their own lives? Did they find a resource they would not otherwise have found? Did they use that resource to their own—not the library's or nonprofit organization's—benefit? Did it produce something notable such as a job interview with a company they might otherwise not have found, or were they able to locate and utilize a service that added to the quality of their own lives? Did the improved customer service itself provide a model that the organization's customers were able to adapt and spread in their own business, volunteer, or community activities?

We certainly cannot pretend that this level of evaluation and documentation is easy or even necessary for every learning opportunity we provide. We would, on the other hand, be underestimating the value to be celebrated if we did not at least consider the possibility that these questions require our attention; they help us understand potential results we may never have considered for all the effort we put into the work we are doing. Those seeking more detailed guidance on using "outcome measurement" within libraries will find plenty of encouragement in *Demonstrating Results,* by Rhea Joyce Rubin, a consultant and former library director who has written extensively about conducting evaluations and measuring results.[2]

Another innovative and inspiring work is *The Six Disciplines of Breakthrough Learning.*[3] This trainer's guide supports the idea that evaluation starts even before the first day of learning—a concept also championed by Robert Brinkerhoff, an educator and consultant whose work is often cited by colleagues managing corporate workplace learning and performance programs.[4] In the *Six Disciplines* model, no one registers for a learning opportunity without first discussing that opportunity with the manager or supervisor who works with the learner; that initial discussion is designed to establish what the learning opportunity offers, what the learner expects to bring back to the workplace, how the manager sees the learning coinciding with the learner's and the organization's goals, and what will be done to support the learner who is returning to the workplace. Using a simple follow-up method described in the book, the authors, for example, were able to document results even at the most elementary level, including a much greater awareness among managers as to what goals their employees were pursuing; 60 percent of the managers who did not use the follow-up were unaware, whereas 100 percent of those using the method had a clear idea of the goals employees were attempting to reach.[5]

Brinkerhoff offers us a sobering appraisal that demonstrates why we should be more concerned with evaluation and anything else that improves the results our efforts produce: 15 percent of those who attend training sessions do not use their learning at all; 15 percent produce "a concrete and valuable result"; and the remaining 70 percent generally use some of what they learn but soon abandon what they acquire because their efforts produce no results or they simply stop trying to apply what they learned.[6] The rhetorical question this produces is, of course, where else other than in training programs would we accept a 15 percent success rate and an 85 percent failure rate?

The follow-up tool described in *Six Disciplines*—Friday5s—is worth examining if we want to alter those dismal results. Once learners complete the formal workshops or courses being offered and then return to their worksites, they engage in weekly follow-up exercises for up to three months. Receiving e-mail each Friday, they spend approximately five minutes documenting what they have accomplished that week by applying what they learned, set goals for what they will accomplish during the following week, and send copies of their responses to their supervisors as well as to those managing the learning process. Although the Friday5s system is an incredibly well-developed tool that has been refined over several years, the concept could easily be adapted for use within any library or nonprofit organization willing to make the commitment to assuring that what is learned does not literally remain abandoned and unused within the physical or virtual classroom but is, instead, nurtured by those who will most benefit from its use. Applying this sort of process to produce and document results reminds us, as the authors quote a corporate leadership training executive saying, that "we are not in the business of providing classes, learning tools, or even learning itself. We are in the business of facilitating improved business results."[7]

A great example of this level of engagement is demonstrated in the North Carolina Master Trainer project, which we describe in more detail in chapter 8. To apply to the program, a staff member must have a letter from the library director stating how the skills learned will be used to benefit the library and its customers. The director must also commit to providing support the staff member needs to be successful in the program—including time away from work to complete Master Trainer projects. Throughout the extensive program, facilitators communicate individually with participants' managers to let them know what changes to look for and expect, and how they can support the participant. The managers are also surveyed periodically to determine what improvements or changes they see on the job as a result of the training.

There is no reason we cannot adapt this belief in libraries and nonprofit organizations so that the goals against which we evaluate success extend beyond providing learning opportunities; we, as leaders, need to embrace the possibility that we facilitate results that ultimately are as meaningful to the customers our organizations serve as they are to the learners themselves. There is also no reason we cannot take the next step recommended by those who have documented results from learners: work to assure that what is learned will actually be supported in the workplace when the learners return. If we are supporting our colleagues' participation in face-to-face or online learning opportunities and working to create the possibility of both formal and informal learning occurring within our organizations, we need to remember that results come from far more than just putting together a great lesson and then moving on to something else. Learners who are not supported in their workplace soon return to their previous behavior if that is what is rewarded.

"The reality is that . . . non-training, performance system factors are the principal determinants of impact from training and can, if they are not aligned and integrated, easily overwhelm even the very best training," Brinkerhoff suggests, and to ignore him is to miss an opportunity worth taking. "Our vast experience in evaluating training programs and the conclusions of many research studies on training transfer and impact all lead to the same conclusions: the principal barriers to achieving greater application of learning and subsequent business results lie in the performance environment of the trainees, not in flaws (though there may be some) in the training programs and interventions themselves."[8]

WHAT OUR COLLEAGUES SAY AND DO

Jay Turner is one of our most diligent colleagues in his pursuit of effective evaluations. He is also one of the few we have encountered who begins planning for the process at the same time he begins planning a workshop or course. He completes at least a rudimentary level of evaluation for every learning opportunity he provides to the staff at the Gwinnett County Public Library.

Discussing how he develops e-learning sessions, he notes that "a success-ful e-learning program corresponds with the library's business drivers, so that it meets a real need. It's not training just for the sake of training." If he is going to include a Level 2 evaluation, he tries to "test the students before, during, and after the program to see if they learned the content":

> If my goal is to have learners walk away with a tangible skill, then an even higher level of feedback is in order. Perhaps I'll test them and then, say, a month later, check in with a random sample of attendees and see if or how they are using their new skill imparted from the e-learning program. I like to wait at least two weeks before doing this level of follow-up to ensure that the halo has worn off and the learning has really taken hold.

It is, he admits, "difficult to get in the habit of higher-level feedback, but there's no other way to know if training is making a difference. I'll be completely honest and say that I don't go to Level 3 and 4 evaluations on everything. It really depends on what business drivers we're trying to address." He does, on the other hand, seek to document those behavioral and result-based elements produced through the Level 3 and Level 4 evaluations for any offering that addresses "any library system-wide performance concern, such as training for policies, guide-lines, and new-hire onboarding: I think it's important to look at learning and development programs as works in progress; you have to continually evaluate your offerings to see if you are hitting your goals for learning and if staff members are truly benefiting from your efforts."

Some of us who are aware of Kirkpatrick's work never get around to engag-ing in his higher levels of engagement simply because we feel we lack the time and do not sense a pressing need for it. Catherine Vaughn, for example, conducts simple evaluations within the Lee County Library System—"but not routinely"—and notes that she has "never been asked or is it expected of me to conduct 'for-mal' evaluations" one or two months after learners have returned to work. She distributes questionnaires to learners, often before a session begins, so they can make notes of positive or negative reactions while a workshop or course is under way. She also informally checks with learners' supervisors to see whether what she offers is making any difference: "I determine success when products are used, e.g., our intranet, the number of complaints has declined because positive comments are up from our customers. . . . The biggest one is when staff aren't as frustrated and don't complain as much—'I don't get it' or 'This is hard to understand,' 'Why did we have to change, the old system was fine.'"

As she considers possibilities, she suggests that she would like to "have each supervisor evaluate their employees on certain skills and topics that were discussed in the workshop that employee recently participated in, and [she] would like to know more about how learners apply lessons to their jobs and what, in learning opportunities, are not meeting their needs."

"At this point," Vaughn continues, "I see that we don't come full circle and that leaves us open to questions like, 'Is this session something we need to be doing or is it to fill time?' 'Can we eliminate this session or do we keep it because we have offered it forever?' 'Are staff learning new skills or improving the ones they have so that it benefits everyone—employees and customers?'"

"I am only one person and am currently stretched in four directions—library CE [continuing education] coordinator, volunteer coordinator, task force facilitator, and County Prepare Training certified instructor," she adds, describing a situation faced by many in library and nonprofit organization training programs.

Other colleagues, reflecting on their use or lack of use of formal evaluations, note that they have tried it both ways. Louise Whitaker regularly conducted evaluations, stopped for a year, and was in the process of reinstituting a revised form of evaluation for the Pioneer Library System when we spoke to her. She took a yearlong hiatus from conducting evaluations because "people were too nice: they never said what they really thought about the training, so everything was always good. Not every training is good; let's be honest. The training doesn't fit everyone's needs all the time, and when they say it [always] does, something is wrong."

The revised form moves Pioneer closer to Kirkpatrick's model:

> We're going to tie the evaluations more immediately after the training and online so they can be anonymous and then follow up with a second evaluation a couple of weeks after the training to see if they're actually using any skills that were talked about during the training. We hope that will give us an idea—if they're not using the skills, is it because there was nothing there that applied to the job, or are they unclear on how to use them?

Jason Puckett, instruction librarian for user education technologies at Georgia State University Library in Atlanta, is among those who readily admit to feeling that they should be doing more to evaluate the effects of learning opportunities: "Part of the problem is that I don't like to take up my very limited class time with evaluation, but then if I'm a guest speaker in someone's class like I often am, I don't have a way to follow up afterward. I'm about to start doing some online workshops and I'll be collecting e-mail addresses to send a follow-up evaluation survey made on SurveyMonkey or something similar."

Rachel Vacek, web services coordinator of the University of Houston Libraries, believes that evaluations are important: "You can't continue to go blindly into the future without having some sense of whether your previous workshops were successful or not." She also, however, cites the same constraints voiced by her Georgia State University Library colleague and says that "sometimes you just want to present information."

Peter Bromberg takes a measured approach to evaluating programs, as shown by his comments about working for the South Jersey Regional Library Cooperative:

> I pay close attention to big events and workshops that we do and I usually do a custom online evaluation form for those events. From the standard paper evaluations, I pretty much want to get a sense of thumbs up or down, why, and what other classes they'd like me to schedule. I'm really not positioned to look closely or monitor whether or not they apply what they've learned in the long term. That's more appropriate at the library level. My big-picture goal is to help library staff acquire the skills and abilities they need to create great customer experiences for the library users of South Jersey.

Reflecting on the efficaciousness of the evaluation form he used, Bromberg says, "The form I use now I pretty much inherited eight years ago. I'm not crazy about it, but I haven't changed it—which," he jokingly added, "gives you some sense of how close attention I pay to the evaluation process."

The question of whether evaluations are necessary and used effectively by organizations leads to some interesting ruminations among those who initially say they believe they should be doing more. Janet Hildebrand, for example, begins by saying that the Contra Costa County Library system does survey staff about training and learning needs and has done follow-up with colleagues involved in special projects such as a computer competency effort: each work unit involved in the project continued to work with team members in the six months following completion of the all-staff trainings. Overall, however, her initial reaction during a discussion about evaluation was that "we're not strong on formal evaluation tools and could do better in this area."

Reflecting on the obvious successes the training program in Contra Costa County produces leads her to suggest that those successes happen because

> this open learning environment, the enthusiasm and participation of so many peer trainers, the verbal articulations of appreciation and amazement from new staff build the trust staff need to continue to

want to learn and therefore they continue to learn and teach others. What comes out of that is a courage to take on new things and an ease of organizational growth and change. So the details matter less, and the testing of learning is not the point really.

She ultimately does agree that there must be some method of accounting for performance as long as learning rather than the testing of learning remains the focus of our efforts: "We are each responsible for our learning. If an individual does not participate, or is not meeting those expectations, then the supervisor must arrange for the training and coaching that the employee needs and requests, and the employee is accountable for his own learning. On that level, we do expect evaluation to be clear, and proactive, and formal."

Because there is no denying the power of a story to suggest success, informal documentation remains an important part of the evaluation process. Turner, for example, recalls offering an online one-on-one session to help a colleague at Gwinnett learn more about using PowerPoint in the workplace if the colleague would share, with others, what she learned:

> At the end of that hour session, this librarian was absolutely stoked. I could hear it in her voice. . . . Months pass. I don't hear much from her, so I naturally assume all is well and that she would reach out to me if she needed any more help. Well, a while later, she asks to borrow my portable projector because she was doing a PowerPoint presentation for her branch. I was ecstatic. She sent me the PowerPoint to review before the presentation and I could see that she used tips we went over in the one-hour session.

Vaughn, in a similar vein, recalls a staff member who attended a reference workshop session on science sources. One month after the workshop, this employee was on a library reference desk when "a frantic mother and her elementary school child came into the library . . . looking for information on manatees and needed a picture also." The staff member remembered learning about the e-resource and was able to provide the information and some pictures that met the child's needs. "The staff member told me that, had it not been for the workshop, she would have just tried the encyclopedia and not thought about e-resources," Vaughn concludes.

Not everyone feels that evaluations are worth the time required to complete them. Management consultant Pat Wagner bluntly states: "Most trainer evaluations are useless. I've given customer service training where the evaluations said it was both the best and worse class people attended. They hated my stories; they loved my stories. The whole process was a waste of time." As a consultant, she needs feedback during the session to make sure she is on track with what the person who hired her wants her to do. "If I get a pile of evaluations three weeks later, what can I do?" she asks.

Wagner suggests that evaluations can be tainted by what motivates a learner to attend a workshop or course. A person who is sent to training and does not really need what is being offered may give a good evaluation because he or she appreciates training, or he or she may give a bad evaluation because attending the training is a waste of time. The person who is sent to training and needs the training may give a good evaluation because he or she likes the instructor's sense of humor or may give a bad evaluation because of a feeling—accurate or inaccurate—that the training is a disciplinary action.

Wagner thinks that the best evaluations come from trained trainers who are in the class. For her, the heart of evaluation is in demonstrating success to the person who hires her. To achieve this, she is explicit from the beginning in outlining the expected outcomes of the training. Because most of her clients are repeat customers, she keeps in touch with them to find out whether they believe her training has been successful.

FULFILLING GREAT EXPECTATIONS

The bottom line is that, as leaders in workplace learning and performance, we need to be prepared to justify our expenses as well as the time and effort required to support our efforts so we can continue to provide learning opportunities to the learners in our organizations; the best way to do this is through measurable outcomes obtained via some form of evaluation and evidence that what we provide has far-reaching and significant effects. We need to have ways of assuring ourselves and those we serve—learners as well as those who benefit from what learners provide and produce—that our resources are not being wasted.

Everyone we interviewed does some form of evaluation, whether formally or informally. There are clearly a wide variety of opinions on using evaluations to measure the success of a training session or program. Furthermore, there is, as Janet Hildebrand suggests, a need to remember that the purpose of conducting evaluations goes far beyond simply testing for learning.

Once we have gathered the information provided through evaluations, we must pay attention to what is done with the data we have generated. If no one is looking at the data and using that information, then we have to wonder whether it is worth the time and effort required to gather it in the first place.

Academic librarians who serve as trainers are particularly challenged when attempting to evaluate their training sessions formally, as Jason Puckett notes. Since most library instruction is offered during the beginning of the semester, there is pressure to do a lot in a limited amount of time. When that constraint is coupled with the fact that academic librarians are reaching out to an audience of students whom they may see only one time, the challenge appears even greater. Puckett sums the challenge up nicely by asking whether even a small part of the single hour he has with his learners should be taken up with evaluations.

The problem we must overcome is that we know evaluations should be done even though many of us are already stretched too thin and wearing too many hats. The irony here is that it is only by conducting effective evaluations that we can gather the data needed to show administrators that training works and that dollars and time spent for learning provide wonderful results. As Peter Bromberg reminds us, our goal is to create great experiences for all who use the services of the organizations we staff. We should expect no less.

NOTES

1. Donald and James Kirkpatrick, *Evaluating Training Programs: The Four Levels* (San Francisco: Berrett-Koehler, 2006).
2. Rhea Joyce Rubin, *Demonstrating Results: Using Outcome Measurement in Your Library* (Chicago: American Library Association, 2006).
3. Calhoun W. Wick, Roy V. H. Pollock, Andrew McK. Jefferson, and Richard D. Flanagan, *The Six Disciplines of Breakthrough Learning: How to Turn Training and Development into Business Results* (San Francisco: Pfeiffer, 2006).
4. Robert O. Brinkerhoff, *Telling Training's Story: Evaluation Made Simple, Credible, and Effective* (San Francisco: Berrett-Koehler, 2006).
5. Wick et al., *Six Disciplines*, 128.
6. Brinkerhoff, *Telling Training's Story*, 19.
7. Wick et al., *Six Disciplines*, 13.
8. Brinkerhoff, *Telling Training's Story*, 38.

8

MASTER TRAINERS, MASTER LEARNERS
TRAINING THE TRAINERS

> One of the most deadly sentences in the English language is
> "I am so glad I am done with school."
>
> —Pat Wagner, Management Consultant and Trainer

F ew of us start our careers with the general goal of becoming a trainer or with the specific goal of becoming a trainer within a library or nonprofit organization. For most of us, this happens as our careers and the needs of the organizations we serve change. "I think people are being thrown into it; I sure was," Louise Whitaker recalls.

Joining colleagues in a master trainer program designed to hone our skills and fill the enormous gaps we find in our own knowledge and experience can, therefore, be exhilarating, challenging, encouraging, and humbling all at the same time. The notification of acceptance into a program conveys with it a certain level of acknowledgment that we are seen as having potential as trainer-teacher-learners. There is also recognition that we have already developed decision-making skills that are of use to those we serve, and that we need to be able to use and improve those skills in moments we are never able to anticipate before they actually occur.

Spending several days together with colleagues in a master trainer program builds and instills a sense of the power of community that might otherwise take months or years to develop—if ever it develops. Working together lesson by lesson, project by project to support and learn from each other increases our skills while also reminding us what our own learners experience as we lead them through learning opportunities. A significant sense of camaraderie develops quickly, accompanied by a sense of responsibility that extends to our classmates, to the organization supporting our participation in the program, to the colleagues who trust that we will share what we have learned, and to ourselves as trainer-teacher-learners in the act of trying to improve ourselves. Immersed for several days in what amounts to an incredibly intense learning lab, we try to fight off all distractions and concentrate on what is being offered. If the process is successful, we and our organizations are transformed positively.

With this in mind, we explore three master trainer programs in this chapter, review the qualities and skills master trainers share, and continue exploring the impacts master trainer programs can and do have according to colleagues throughout the United States.

MASTER TRAINERS IN NORTH CAROLINA

For more than a decade the State Library of North Carolina has offered its Master Trainer certification program. The program is well respected and highly thought of in the North Carolina community and other parts of the country. Its master trainers are sought to conduct training for libraries across the state—both in person and virtually through webinars.

The program, funded by a federal IMLS/LSTA (Institute of Museum and Library Services/Library Services and Technology Act) grant, is one of the most successful curriculums ever initiated by the state library. It features a competitive process, with those interested in participating required to complete an application and have a letter of recommendation from their library director. When the final class is selected, public and academic libraries from the Blue Ridge Mountains to the Outer Banks are represented.

The Master Trainer program began in 1997 and has had more than one hundred graduates. The program began when state librarian Sandy Cooper saw a dramatic need for training resulting from the influx of computer-related technology in libraries. At that time, not every library had a computer, state library continuing education consultant Raye Oldham says. The need for the program has continued, and the focus has changed from technology to instructional design. Initially the program comprised classes exclusively for academic librarians or exclusively for public librarians. But, according to Oldham, they quickly recognized a need for a mix within each class: "We're blending the types of libraries so they can learn from each other and see what they have in common."

During its first ten years of operation, the program has changed to incorporate e-learning, so face-to-face time between instructors and students has decreased. It began as a three-part, nine-day program. The first segment consisted of a five-day boot camp for library staff where participants learned the basics of training design and learning theories and split into groups for practice teaching. The second segment was a three-day session in which each participant delivered a one-hour presentation in front of the other participants. The final segment was a single-day "Trainers' Showcase" where trainers could present in front of peers and library directors from across the state.

The program now begins with synchronous and asynchronous training sessions followed by a four-day segment. After a brief introduction, instructor Margery Orell tells participants that they will earn the equivalent of a master's degree during their subsequent months together. By the end of the first week, participants in small groups develop and present a one-hour training session on a topic of their choice. They are evaluated not only by the program's facilitators but by their peers.

There are four months of work between the first and second sessions; participants strive within their own libraries to develop and present the one-hour training program, and there are online coaching sessions. Participants then reconvene for the three-day session that consists of a day of review and more learning, the training showcase and graduation ceremony, and a third day of feedback and evaluations.

Oldham says the showcase has remained an important part of the program for both participants and their directors: "It's similar to what parents experience with a science fair or graduation, not to see the individual work but within the context of the larger group and to see their trainer spotlighted. It's a positive experience that you can't really achieve in another way."

MASTER TRAINERS IN NEW JERSEY

The New Jersey Train-the-Trainer project, a New Jersey State Library–sponsored program that has graduated more than 270 participants since being organized in the late 1990s, is a far more concentrated effort than that offered in North Carolina. Participants, with a goal of creating training plans they can use within their own organizations, gather for three consecutive days of work, separate for a week, then reconvene for a fourth day that includes time for participants to deliver presentations drawn from what they have developed through the workshop. The program offers 30 hours of continuing education credit.

Before they meet for the first time, participants complete online forms including a learning style profile that explores how they prefer to solve problems; how they prefer to interact in group discussions; and how they prefer to learn material they are studying. They also complete an instructional styles diagnosis inventory that gives them an opportunity to explore how they prefer to conduct themselves when they are instructing other adults.

"The ultimate goal of the NJTTT workshop is that participants will learn how to develop and conduct effective training," Peter Bromberg, who participated as a learner and remained active as an organizer and presenter, has written. "This model has helped create a tight-knit community of trainers who come from libraries of all types, and all geographic regions across the state."[1]

During their time together, participants are exposed to and work with a variety of themes including how to use adult learning principles, developing learning objectives, selecting training methods and training aids, working in electronic classrooms, developing lesson plans, honing facilitation and presentation skills, and evaluating training programs. Comments from participants are tremendously enthusiastic, Bromberg reports.

The planners took a two-year hiatus beginning in 2007 to completely reorganize what was being offered; the new version, first offered in 2009, is much more technology rich and continues to attract committed and energetic participants who have been involved in training programs but arrive with "little or no formal background in the art of training adults," according to Bromberg. "The Train-the-Trainer program was invaluable," he says. "It gave me the theory and foundation I needed to become a good trainer. I couldn't recommend it more highly." Although New Jersey libraries received devastating cuts at the state level in 2010, we were happy to see that the Train-the-Trainer program is still listed as a high priority for 2011.

MASTER TRAINERS IN CALIFORNIA

Drawing from the North Carolina and New Jersey examples, the California-based Infopeople project organized a four-day Master Trainer program in 2002 and invited representatives from fourteen of the state's largest library systems to participate at no charge to the libraries. It was, for those who participated, a transformative experience at many levels. It provided the sort of well-balanced curriculum offered in North Carolina and New Jersey; included time, on the first day, for the trainers and administrators from library systems in Northern and

Southern California as well as Central California Valley communities to interact and discuss training successes and training needs; and included a variety of exercises and opportunities to develop a learning community designed to last far longer than the four-day program itself.

Broad topics covered throughout the program included defining the term *master trainer* to denote those who are continually engaged in improving their skills and engaged in learning, are willing to take risks and set high goals for themselves and their organizations, and are willing to try new techniques in their workplace learning and performance efforts. The program continued with in-depth explorations of how to conduct needs assessments and evaluations, design and develop effective lessons, deliver effective learning opportunities, and spread innovation throughout an organization. The culminating experience of delivering a presentation common to other master trainer programs was replicated in the Infopeople offering; program participants delivered five-minute presentations that were video taped so they would have yet another tool to help them improve the skills they already possessed or were in the process of developing. Participants also left the program with a binder full of training materials that continues to serve as a ready reference source for those of us who retained or have access to it.

Infopeople sought innovative ways to keep the program alive while trying to organize a new master trainer cohort: components of the four-day training were offered as one-day stand-alone workshops throughout the state, and the organization posted some of its training materials within its online archives for those who wanted to draw from what had been developed. An attempt to update the curriculum formally and create a second cohort of master trainers throughout California ended in autumn 2008 when budget constraints put the project on hold.

LEARNING THAT CONTINUES TO SPREAD

The learning gained in each of the three master trainer programs reviewed above does not end with graduation, as it does with so many other types of education and workplace learning and performance efforts. The leadership skills enhanced through these programs are supported by those who sponsor the sessions; there is also continuing contact and collaboration among the trainers themselves.

North Carolina Master Trainers are grouped into regional subgroups that meet regularly to discuss and create new training. Graduates are also part of the statewide Master Trainers electronic discussion list. Lydia Towery, librarian at the Charlotte Mecklenburg Library and graduate of the 1998 Master Trainer program, says that one of the most beneficial aspects of the program is the opportunity to network with other trainers. It is a benefit to be able to send an e-mail to the discussion list or call a fellow Master Trainer program participant on the phone and mention the cycle of learning to others sharing that common language.

Raye Oldham says that once participants complete the program, they often are promoted in their own library or hired by another library or organization, but even this has potential benefits to the entire library and nonprofit workplace learning industry; as those of us who graduate from master trainer programs move into new positions, we encounter colleagues with similar experiences and continue to learn—and share what we learn—in increasingly diffused communities of learners, including the ALA's training group (the ALA Learning Round Table) and ASTD. Oldham is not aware of any other state library system that offers a comprehensive training program comparable to what has been created in North Carolina.

The New Jersey program has also documented successful outcomes, according to Peter Bromberg: "This model has helped create a tight-knit community of trainers who come from libraries of all types, and all geographic regions across the state. In any given year we may have from seven to fifteen trainers, and another five to ten graduates who understudy lessons, help plan, and/or attend a day or two of training as observers and offer structured feedback to trainers."[2]

There were numerous attempts by Infopeople to build upon its initial successes. Its program graduates were encouraged to post new resources on a shared site maintained by Infopeople, remain in touch via a discussion list, and take initiative in letting Infopeople representatives know what they could do to support the trainers once they had returned to their own organizations. Although Infopeople was unable to obtain funding through the California state library to repeat the comprehensive four-day workshop to form a second cohort of master trainers—which suggests that if we expect to see more programs along these lines we must be creative in establishing sustainable long-term funding sources—annual reunions for those who attended continued for a few years. The annual gatherings alternated between the Los Angeles and San Francisco Bay areas so the group would retain its statewide presence. As the cohort of original participants dwindled—many moved into other positions within their organizations or within other organizations—the reunion sessions remained open to people who had moved into training positions within the original fourteen library systems. Although the final formal reunion was held in 2006, some of the original participants and their successors remain in contact with each other, and a few have become involved with Infopeople in other capacities.

LEARNING FROM THE LESSONS
WE ARE OFFERED

Some of the best lessons we have acquired through participation in a master trainer program come from unexpectedly having to apply what we were being taught. One of us, for example, had to withdraw from a master trainer program because of complications from a pregnancy and later start again from the beginning. (We'll let you figure out which one of us that was.) The obvious lesson learned and applied was that learning is sometimes significantly affected by unexpected circumstances, and this is a lesson any of us can recall and use effectively when our own students' personal challenges interfere with their ability to complete the assignments.

One of us—the one who was not affected by a pregnancy—had a similarly unexpected and sobering learning experience while attending Infopeople's four-day Master Trainer program. Preparations for the culminating final presentation were interrupted by the news that a close family member had been rushed to a hospital for emergency surgery. There was the immediate dilemma to resolve: withdraw from the final day of the program to be at the relative's bedside, or remain onsite at the program and deliver the presentation as scheduled. The decision to remain onsite and finish the program—fully supported by the relative—offered one of the most important lessons acquired: although there is no clear right or wrong answer in this sort of situation, whatever decision is made becomes the right one at that moment, and we discover amazing reservoirs of strength and support within ourselves and those who surround us. We also discover that decisions made with that incredible level of support prepare us for many of the easier decisions—as well as even more difficult ones—we face in nearly every task we undertake.

Though we certainly hope that those of you reading these lines do not find your master trainer experiences taking you down these particular paths, we can assure you that whatever you do experience can somehow be turned to your benefit if you are willing to apply what you are learning, make the decision that is best for you, and find a way to integrate that experience into your own best practices as you continue in your role of trainer-as-leader.

THE PREPARATION THAT TRAINERS
TYPICALLY DO (OR DO NOT) RECEIVE

Few of our colleagues in libraries recall having received formal training before beginning to serve as trainers or workplace learning and performance program managers—which is a shame since there certainly are options, including workshops through ASTD, instructional design programs at colleges and universities, e-learning certificate programs through a variety of sources including the eLearning Guild, and an increasingly varied set of online offerings through webinars and other online courses.

Much of what we use in our day-to-day work is what we have picked up along the way. We continue to acquire skills and knowledge and seek fast ways to fill the gaps through a variety of options: those rare master trainer programs, the increasingly common webinars, half- or full-day workshops, conferences, and brief or semester-long online courses. Those of us who reach the point where we see no other option are immersing ourselves in certification programs such as ASTD's Certified Professional in Learning and Performance offering or making the commitment to return to graduate-level coursework while keeping up with our full-time occupations. In this way, we are able to enhance skills that are beginning to feel more than a little bit outdated, and we receive useful and effective reminders of what our own learners experience when they engage in lifelong learning.

Jay Turner, one of our colleagues who did have formal training before accepting the position he holds at Gwinnett County, recalls attending a weeklong train-the-trainer program hosted by Georgia Public Library Service "several years ago, before I was a training manager," and he has also attended the Train-the-Trainer Boot Camp offered by the Bob Pike Group. "I'm a firm believer that professionals should be credentialed in their specialties," he notes.

> I think all workplace learning leaders should go through a full-blown train-the-trainer program, and that a version of it—something less time intensive and more tailored for the job—could be offered to other levels of staff who are not necessarily workplace learning and performance leaders. . . . Who wants to be taught by someone who comes across amateurish? Definitely not me. At Gwinnett, most members of our training team have attended what I consider the core pieces of Pike's Train-the-Trainer Boot Camp.
>
> To make such a program a reality, organizations have to be willing to devote resources to improving their learning and developmental efforts by investing in their learning and performance pros. This could include providing funding for these professionals to attend outside master trainer programs, or providing the time and funding for your own staff to develop such a program in house.

More common among trainers is the experience Jason Puckett describes while recalling the first library instruction class he offered to a group of freshman at Emory University:

> I was terrified. I wore a tie in the hope that it might make them treat me with more respect. I did that for about the first year—wore a tie whenever I was teaching. It was my security blanket. They were completely bored. I knew the subject matter I was trying to teach them but had no idea how to present it in a way that would be the slightest bit engaging or interesting. I just demonstrated the process and was relieved it was over.

Puckett later received formal training on how to teach when he began earning his MLIS and took one class on library instruction. "I would have taken more [classes] if they had more," Puckett says. "We worked on actual course planning and were required to find a venue to teach them. This is where I learned a lot about learning theory, planning outcomes, learning styles and so on, a lot of the theoretical stuff that I think has helped me pin down why some teaching techniques work better than others and helped me expand my repertoire."

Pat Wagner was only sixteen years old when she gave her first training session. Her high school journalism department won an award and as a result she attended a national secondary school journalism conference. Wagner gave a presentation on how to research and prepare feature stories for school newspapers to an auditorium full of high school students attending the conference. The presentation was an hour long and, though it was exhilarating, she had terrible stage fright, she remembers. When asked why she gave such a presentation, Wagner said it was out of respect for her journalism teacher and the realization that she had something to offer. Wagner's lesson learned was, "You can't wait until you are perfect and you can't wait until fear goes away."

SKILLS AND QUALITIES OF A MASTER TRAINER

The Infopeople Master Trainer sessions offered explicit guidance to those attempting to define master trainer skills: subject matter expertise, design and development experience, the ability to produce effective materials for learners, communication and theatrical skills, and a cool head and warm heart. Addressing the subject of expertise, Louise Whitaker notes that not all trainers need to be experts in every subject they teach:

When you're standing up in front of a group, at that particular moment you're the expert because most people there are not going to know as much as you know. Rather than feeling that you don't know what you're doing, you go into it with a different mindset. I think it's also important for the trainer to be open to learning. It's amazing the number of times in a session that someone says something and you say, "Oh, I didn't know that" or "I didn't think of that." You can learn from them as easily as they learn from you.

Among the critically important traits great trainers bring to learners is a sense of enthusiasm, Denver Public's Sandra Smith suggests. Trainers should be "enthusiastic if not passionate." They also should be "open and friendly," "connect with people on an interpersonal level," "convey that they are interested in the attendees' interest" in the topics being explored, and "feel a commitment" to the topics as well as the importance of the topics to the organizations and customers being served. She also advocates being adept at time management, having strong skills to organize material being offered to learners, having an ability to communicate effectively to groups as well as to individuals, being proactive in solving problems and in the overall process of serving as a trainer, and understanding that learners may be at different stages of acquiring knowledge even though they are all attending a workshop designed to move attendees from one pre-specified skill level to another."

"In almost any training, you're going to have people at different levels," Whitaker agrees. "You have to be patient with the person at the bottom rung or they're going to feel that they're a disruption, that they shouldn't be in there, so I think it's important to recognize that not everyone that is in a training is going to have the same skills. That's frustrating sometimes."

"Thinking on your feet is important," Jason Puckett says. "Being willing to take risks in front of a room full of people. Being able to put yourself in the position of the learner." "I'm having a rather humbling experience at work right now learning some responsibilities in a completely new area to me," he notes. "I'm completely lost at the moment and trying to remember this feeling for the next time I get impatient with a student who isn't getting what seems very obvious to me."

Our own experience confirms what Puckett suggests, and we have even found that taking similar courses in two different settings can be invaluable. Having learned in a frustrating and ill-defined course, then learning the same material from well-organized and inspirational instructors brings to the trainer-teacher-learner in all of us a lesson learned viscerally and one we can replicate for those we serve.

"Being honest about what you don't know" is also important, according to Puckett. "When I was less secure as a teacher, I was afraid of the questions I couldn't answer. Now I find I'm a lot more comfortable saying, 'I don't know, let's try it and see,' or 'I don't know, e-mail me after class and I'll figure it out.' Nobody expects you to know everything, and it took me a surprisingly long time to learn that."

Patience also is high on the list of qualities cited by Janet Hildebrand: "Patience, understanding, ability to 'read' the specific learner and put themselves in that learner's place, desire to help the other person be successful, ability to articulate clearly, a sense of fun about learning" are all among the elements she and her colleagues seek among trainers at the Contra Costa County Library system. "Actual depth of expertise may not always be the most important trait, but rather knowing enough to be ahead of the learner and not afraid to not know everything—to be still learning oneself" are also important, she continues.

Although Hildebrand and her colleagues do look for employees and prospective employees who already display many of these skills and qualities, they are also open to working "with those who want to and who volunteer and have potential to develop into good trainers," she says, noting that an organization with this philosophy "begins to develop an environment where this kind of learning and helping each other is the norm; when you look around, everyone is doing it, and they are enjoying their relationship and connectivity with each other, and they are all feeling successful . . . It may take a few years, but that's how it comes about."

An interest in continuing education is essential, Pat Wagner says. Noting that learners frequently approach her after training sessions and ask how they can do what she is doing, she says her first response is, "What are you reading? If you want to be a trainer, what are you reading about training?" She is surprised by the large number of librarians who consult her or other trainers for resources before even searching their own collections. Wagner, in a constant attempt to gain new information, has acquired more than three thousand books and offers no hint that she is finished adding to her collection. "One of the most deadly sentences in the English language is 'I am so glad I am done with school,'" she suggests. In her consulting practice, she wants people to have the richness and complexity of a postgraduate college class, so she strives to learn as much as she can about a variety of topics.

Returning to the theme of what train-the-trainer programs should inspire and provide, Jay Turner suggests "presentation skills—face-to-face and live online; assessing needs, developing courses; evaluating training initiatives; working with problem participants or exceptional learners; effective use of props, visuals, and classroom technology; [and] developing effective job aids. I'll also say that, with the proliferation of e-learning, I'd love to see a separate train-the-trainer program for e-learning."

QUALITIES AND PASSION

It is clear that there are particular personal qualities that help workplace learning and performance leaders succeed within libraries and nonprofit organizations. Having a passion for learning and sharing that love of learning top the list, but other valuable qualities can be cultivated during our careers. The ability to think on our feet in order to troubleshoot technological and other problems during a learning session is helpful. Demonstrating patience and empathy with learners who may be apprehensive or shy is another key quality. The ability to balance confidence with humility remains important for any trainer. Being self-motivated as well as flexible helps in the ever-changing field of workplace learning and performance. It is also important to be enthusiastic about what we do. As trainer-learner-leaders, if we are not enthusiastic about what we are doing, it is obvious to our learners.

To make workplace learning and performance programs as good as they can be, organizations have to be willing to devote resources to improving their offerings by investing in their learning and performance leaders. This could include providing funding for these professionals to attend outside master trainer programs or providing the time and funding for other members of staff to develop such a program in-house.

The good news is that this dichotomy does not exist in the Gwinnett County Public Library system and other first-rate organizations. Jay Turner says administrators at Gwinnett support his attendance at off-site training sessions, display an understanding that administrative leave and fees to attend learning opportunities are a direct investment in the library's staff development program, and take pride in being on the cutting edge of library services. Maintaining an innovative employee development program is just one of the ways the library works to achieve its goals.

It is obvious that not all libraries and nonprofit organizations are this fortunate, so we agree with Turner's assertion that workplace learning and performance leaders have to be master salespeople as well as master trainers. As Turner says, we need to look for opportunities to demonstrate how we are incorporating into our work the concepts from seminars we attend and to paint the picture of how our efforts tangibly help our organizations meet their goals and implement their mission, vision, and value statements. Furthermore, as we suggest in chapter 7 and Turner says in conversations, we need a long-range view of how what we provide ultimately serves the needs of the library members and guests we serve and the larger communities in which they operate.

It is not, as Peter Bromberg notes, enough to "just grab someone and say, 'You're training this workshop' and expect them to do a good job. . . . Generally speaking, one doesn't become a good artist, good musician, good ball player, or good mathematician without some training." As leaders, we need to argue for more and make the sustained efforts required to produce the magnificent results we should expect from trainers who are masters at their craft.

NOTES

1. Peter Bromberg, "New Jersey's Train-the-Trainer: Creating a Community of Library Instructors," 2004, www.sjrlc.org/ttt.htm.
2. Ibid.

9

THE END IS THE BEGINNING
LEADERSHIP AND LEARNING
IN AN ONSITE-ONLINE WORLD

If you quit learning, you quit living.

—Catherine Vaughn, Continuing
Education Coordinator, Lee
County Library System

s we look for additional ways to improve our own skills to the benefit of those relying on us, all of us as current or prospective learning leaders need to acknowledge that we are in the middle of a major change in the way we train, learn, lead, collaborate, and conduct business as well as social matters.[1] Our first, second, and third places—home, work, and social gathering sites, as described by Ray Oldenburg in *The Great Good Place*—are increasingly overlapping and extending into those proposed fourth places: social learning centers.[2] Concurrently, more and more of us are learning to operate face-to-face and online; we recognize that the time of either/or choices implied by questions such as "should we work on-site or online?" has already disappeared for many and is disappearing for many more.[3] The question of which social networking tools to use is really as ephemeral as the tools themselves have become;[4] what is important is that we are working where our colleagues are working, and we need to move from tool to tool as our colleagues quickly move to take advantage of the opportunities that are attracting many of us.

What remains constant is that learning is at the center of much of what we do. It is up to us to decide whether we want to lead in this important endeavor or let others set the agenda.

We also have to recognize the importance of looking beyond the physical and virtual borders of the organizations we serve, as many of our colleagues concur; remind ourselves of why we were—and remain—attracted to workplace learning and performance; and remember to continue dreaming.

STEPPING OUT

The simple act of moving physically or virtually outside our own buildings inspires and rejuvenates us. It is the first step in avoiding staleness in our approach, Lee County Library System continuing education coordinator Catherine Vaughn suggests. "I get the following out of attending workshops, webinars, etc.: reinforcement of my ideas. Sometimes I think to myself, 'Gee, am I going down the right path? Were my thoughts in the ball park?' I also walk away with ideas I had not thought about on my own or a different way of delivering or adding to what I have done in the past."

There is more, she says: "I also form bonds with fellow instructors so I can get additional information from them. I find I do this more on the local level but do it nonetheless. I especially love it when someone liked an idea I had and they want more info from me."

Working closely with the training coordinator for the entire county provides even more support and inspiration, she says: "We bounce ideas back and forth, and I've given her some of my materials to use in developing sessions for our county."

Attending conferences and being active in professional associations during good economic times are among the external resources Vaughn values: "Before the economy plunged, I went to the ALA and ASTD conferences on a regular basis. It is great to see familiar faces and discuss ideas with people going through the challenges. I network with library members through our library consortium, SWFLN [Southwest Florida Library Network], and that helps me stay up with other library organizations. I also serve on the Continuing Education Committee for SWFLN and offer my advice as well as take suggestions from neighboring libraries."

Even becoming a member of these nonprofit organizations and their local affiliates leads to additional opportunities to extend our communities of learning. Members of ASTD chapters—those local affiliates of a nonprofit workplace learning and performance organization with national and international connections—find that moving beyond the walls of their local meeting rooms connects them to resources that would otherwise be unavailable. Those opportunities include service on task forces as well as on national committees and advisory groups that meet face-to-face as well as online. Their successes, furthermore, are documented, celebrated, and shared online through sites including ASTD's Share Our Success (SOS) page—which then serves as yet another example of all that ASTD members produce and disseminate to the benefit of those they reach.[5]

Vaughn and other ASTD supporters are not alone in cherishing those outside activities, relationships, and resources. "It has been extremely valuable to me to get out of my place of employment and visit other libraries, and converse with colleagues," Princeton Public Library assistant director Peter Bromberg says. "Last week, I had the pleasure of visiting the Allen County Public Library in Fort Wayne, Indiana—a wonderful library, by the way, that is well worth visiting! Within two hours of my visit, my mind was racing with new ideas and new perspectives that have helped me creatively address challenges in my current workplace."

Bromberg also visited that library "for a one-day unconference called 'Library Camp,' where [he] got to hear from and converse with so many smart, creative people:

> For me, there is no substitute for that experience. There is almost something magical about removing myself from my daily environment, my daily routines, and my daily relationships and interacting with a variety of people in the context of learning and sharing. It is simply one of the most useful and productive experiences I have in my professional life. So, to sum up: I think it has been absolutely vital for my learning and effectiveness to get out of the building once in a while.

Denver Public Library learning and development manager Sandra Smith speaks with equal passion of moving outside her organization to "seek out and receive new info and connections, mentally and physically, that can stimulate our thinking about what we do. Also, going to events gives me new ideas, information, and techniques that can be useful and often have been tried by others, so that I'm getting best practices—saving me time in not reinventing the wheel, and giving me new paths to follow."

"It is too easy to get stuck in neutral and not even realize it," Pioneer Library System training coordinator Louise Whitaker agrees. "I need to be willing to explore new ideas and be exposed to different ways of doing things. That won't happen if I don't interact with colleagues."

Though more and more of us are taking advantage of opportunities to make and sustain outside connections through online social networking tools, there remains a real need for those face-to-face encounters that Bromberg, Smith, and

Whitaker appropriately praise. "I'm a huge proponent of meeting online—it's convenient and saves money. However, even with all the online collaboration tools available, I still find value in meeting colleagues face-to-face," Gwinnett County Public Library training manager Jay Turner agrees. "There's something about connecting physically: beyond getting energized by the good vibes of friends, I usually find that extemporaneous conversations begin that go off in amazing directions, often sparking my creativity or giving me an opportunity to ignite someone else's."

For the two of us who have written this book, the combination of online and face-to-face interactions has followed a pattern we increasingly are noticing. We first met through an online exchange when one of us responded to the other's blog posting about master trainer programs. We exchange ideas online using everything from online chat and VoIP tools to resources that allow us to share and edit documents synchronously as well as asynchronously—large sections of this book, for example, were prepared through the use of Google Docs and Dropbox. We exchange information via the U.S. Postal Service and phone calls; meet face-to-face at conferences held throughout the country and occasionally have the pleasure of preparing presentations online and then offering them at the conferences we attend; participate in online meetings of the groups to which we and our colleagues belong; and even take advantage of those rare times when a little extra travel time puts us in the same place at the same time.

The variety of meeting places continues to offer "and" rather than "either/or" choices, and conferences and workshops remain instrumental in our development, the development of our colleagues, and the development of various organizations. "One of the best benefits I've gained from attending a specific workshop was participating in [workplace learning and performance author, presenter, researcher, and analyst] Elliott Masie's Extreme Learning Lab back in 2007," Turner says:

> I spent close to a week at Masie's lab . . . exploring what were, at the time, some amazing new technologies that Masie believed would shape learning and training for years to come. . . . I had an opportunity to try out several rapid-authoring tools I'd never used before; this was before I owned Captivate and Articulate Studio. I had a chance to try some well-crafted simulations from the army as well as try to create a few simple simulations of my own. I also met some of the brightest minds in training, including Bob Mosher—a Microsoft expatriate who's perhaps the biggest name in electronic performance support systems. I half-jokingly tell people that the Extreme Learning Lab gave me about five years worth of fodder for me to futurize my library's

training program. . . . That event was worth at least triple the $1,500 registration fee.

Masie's lab was also Turner's "formal introduction to creating online learning and considering virtual worlds for training"—a talent that is unsurpassed among those we know who are currently working in library and nonprofit workplace learning and performance programs. He elaborates:

> What I knew of e-learning and virtual worlds before then was from my own independent study during my days of interning in my library's training department . . . before I was training manager. During that time, I was transitioning from undergrad to grad school, and much of my work and collaboration was online. The latent interest was there, and I was fortunate to be working in an environment where I could somewhat explore my personal interests, even though it was not part of my day-to-day work. . . . the learning lab was the formal introduction, but as with a lot of the development of ideas that I use for training and e-learning it comes from a lot of personal interest and exploration— often on my own time.

He also recalls, with gratitude, the presentation skills he acquired while attending Bob Pike's workshops. Among the topics covered were managing a classroom, facilitation techniques, and preparing content. "What I found most valuable were some subtle methods for altering my stage approach to best fit my audience. I'm not a pro presenter at this point in my career by a long shot"—a point with which many of us would strongly disagree—"but I believe this work-shop really helped shape me into one that is more polished and has the ability to work with groups of various compositions, from line staff to mangers to directors."

Whitaker also notes how much she has gained through interactions with her peers at conferences:

> Attending a session at [the annual] ALA [conference] on becoming a learning organization . . . made me realize that it should be more learner driven. At ALA this past summer, it was great to attend sessions on online learning to see what other libraries are doing and how we can improve our products, since we are just beginning to develop our own online modules.
>
> For online training, I am excited about getting some assistance— guidance—from Jay Turner. I want to be as good as he when I grow up. The other person would be Sandra Smith in Denver. It is good to

see what others are doing and steal ideas. From Jay, I am getting help with spiffying up our presentations with animation and making them more interactive and interesting. Informative is important, but they also need to be at least a little entertaining. From Sandra, just ideas on different trainings that they offer that we might consider incorporating.

Sometimes stepping out does not have to involve going very far, as Char Booth, e-learning librarian at the University of California–Berkeley's University Library, concurs:

> I also lead trainings and workshops outside of my immediate library organization. I managed to build a strong relationship with the campus Educational Technology Services (ETS) unit and started leading library/information-related faculty and staff trainings on our campus learning management system, bSpace, in the ETS training facility. It took a long while to establish my credibility with them as a teacher, and it has been a very gratifying and successful collaboration. It has also been interesting to learn to train in a different "language," so to speak, by working within their information paradigm and outside the library paradigm for a change.

STEPPING OUT EVEN MORE

As leaders, we clearly need to model the behavior we are promoting. It is not enough to provide others with the learning opportunities they need. As should be clear from much of what we and our colleagues have said through the comments at the heart of this book, we need to educate ourselves continually for a variety of reasons. We must stay at least a few steps ahead of those we serve; remain viscerally connected to the experience of being a learner so we can deliver the best of what we experience; and avoid, with an almost fanatical commitment, what has discouraged or prevented us from learning. We also recognize the importance of immersing ourselves in classic and contemporary literature, not only in the field of workplace learning and performance but in innovation and change theory, in the fields in which we work and play, and in areas of practice that appear to have no connection to what we do but add to the richness of our knowledge and the depth of all we offer.

The two of us, for example, returned to formal academic programs to earn degrees while this book was in progress, and our experiences have helped shape the questions we asked our colleagues and the material we chose to include.

The distance-learning aspects of our education, furthermore, helped us viscerally understand the pleasures and challenges students of all ages face as delivery methods for training-teaching-learning continue to evolve.

Our involvement in a variety of local, regional, national, and international organizations and activities have further added to what we are able to offer others.

We have also, through our continuing education, our own curiosity, and face-to-face and online interchanges with our colleagues, continued steeping ourselves in the literature of leadership by reading everything we can find, from Kouzes and Posner's *Leadership Challenge* to the latest publications released by ASTD.[6] We continue to look to well-respected classics in the field of change management, including Rogers's *Diffusion of Innovations,* as well as to more recent releases including the Heath brothers' entertaining and change-inducing *Switch.*[7] We turn to Knowles's *Adult Learner* and Senge's *Fifth Discipline.*[8] Where training-teaching-learning is concerned, the synthesis of work and play and learning could not be more complete.

Participating in our in-house and external communities of learning provides a constant flow of ideas—either new or those we have already encountered but failed to assimilate and use effectively—and reminds all of us that, no matter how isolated we may sometimes feel, we really never are alone.

NURTURING THOSE OUTSIDE CONTACTS

For many of us, there can never be enough contact with the colleagues who help us do our work better. "I'm in continual contact with a great network of talented people through a variety of channels including IM, Twitter, Facebook, e-mail, and phone," Peter Bromberg notes. "IM has been particularly useful. Do I wish I had more time for such contacts? If you'd asked me four months ago, I would have said, 'no—I have enough time.' But since I've started a new job recently, it does seem like I've dropped out of the stream a bit and have only just recently started to reconnect with people."

CREATING AND LIVING
WITHIN THE INTERSECTION

That we need to improve our ability to create a balance between doing our job and maintaining contact with colleagues within and outside our own organizations is both an issue we need to consider and, at a larger level, one that creates an artificial dilemma akin to the issue of balancing work with training and learning. On the one hand, we recognize that we become better at what we do through the "Intersection" created when people from different places or backgrounds briefly meet and disperse to disseminate what they developed together, which Frans Johansson describes so well in *The Medici Effect*.[9] On the other hand, treating these Intersection moments as anything less than an integral part of the work we do as trainer-teacher-learners makes us miss a basic point: learning is a part of everyone's job, and organizations that see training and learning as frills are dooming themselves to mediocrity and the flight of their most innovative and valuable leaders and prospective leaders.

Management consultant and trainer Pat Wagner adds nuance to this assertion as she discusses the word *colleague* and what it means to be in contact with colleagues outside our own organizations: "Potentially, everyone is a colleague, and sometimes what happens is someone gets trained in a certain way and has certain credentials, and that's who they hang out with. What I'm interested in . . . is that when we're talking about human behavior, there are so many fields and disciplines in the world. Who are you hanging out with? Are you listening to anthropology professors? Are you hanging out with dog trainers?"

The wider our range of contacts, she continues, the more likely we are to not be limited to the conventional thinking of those within our own field of practice and experience: "For example, if your focus is on adult education, you might want to make friends with psychologists. . . . if you are a very practical person, it might be nice to make friends with academics who know more theory. Whatever your box, you want to make more contacts, formal and informal, outside of that box, face-to-face and online, but nothing substitutes for face-to-face."

An additional value to stepping into the Intersection that occurs when members of various communities meet and exchange ideas, she says, is that it prevents us from being complacent: "The question for someone like me, then, is: how do I keep from degenerating into somebody who is smug, complacent, feels entitled, [and] is too tired to learn anymore? I have to be really, really careful about having enough people around me telling the truth."

Because, as Wagner suggests, some of the most interesting colleagues we encounter are from fields other than our own, those of us working in libraries and nonprofit organizations have the built-in advantage of continually and with little effort being exposed to ideas from widely diverse segments of our small and large face-to-face and online communities simply because the nature of our work draws us all together. If we ignore the value and the possibilities this collaboration can provide, we not only cheat ourselves, we cheat those who rely on us to provide a broad-based program of learning opportunities that contributes to the overall development of the various and overlapping communities we encounter and are serving.

DREAMING

To bring a smile to the faces of those involved in training-teaching-learning within libraries and nonprofit organizations, ask us to dream. We are full of dreams, and some of us are actually good at bringing people together to move from dreams to action. As we concluded the interviews for this book, we asked our colleagues what their workplace learning and performance programs would include if they had unlimited resources.

Playfulness was at the top of Jay Turner's dream list, and this is an element that appeals to many of us. "I wish that all learners in my library had access to a sandbox," he admits. "I try to build time and request resources that allow me to have a functioning digital sandbox—a place where I can explore ideas and tools to improve the e-learning portion of the training I do at Gwinnett County Public Library."

Turner's suggestion creates an interesting vision akin to what Google offers its employees by encouraging them to pursue their own interests at least 20 percent of the time they are working. If each workplace had the equivalent of its own learning sandbox—a place where staff could go and simply explore innovative ideas and tech tools during predetermined times—we might see an explosion of personal and professional growth that helped them better serve customers and meet other aspects of their organization's strategic and business plans. The Charlotte Mecklenburg Library saw this briefly as staff participated in the 23 Things program.

Peter Bromberg offers a variation on the theme of learning supported by the organizations we, in turn, support:

> I think the biggest challenge for workplace learning and performance improvement is time, so if resources were unlimited, I'd like to have more staff—which would allow all staff to have more time to do self-directed learning. I'd also like some of that free time to be used for staff to get together and present to each other on topics that they have learned about and/or are interested in. . . . I'd also like to hire someone to coordinate staff development and learning—someone creative, with an ability to see the big picture and an ability to create interesting, engaging learning experiences. . . . You can't legislate that behavior. It flows from the culture of an organization.

Catherine Vaughn offers her own ideas on playfulness and innovation:

> I would have the sessions I have in place but offer them in different formats. I would offer my library orientation as a bus tour—I did do that in the past but had to stop due to dwindling resources. We toured numerous libraries including our processing center, Talking Books library, our Bookmobile, and the administration offices. We had a boxed lunch to keep everyone together and just spent eight hours together, learning about our library system and each other.

That program, which Vaughn developed, received national recognition through an ALA H. W. Wilson Library Staff Development Grant, which is given to one library system each year "for a program of staff development designed to further the goals and objectives of the library organization."[10]

Vaughn also dreams of increasing what she offers through experiential learning:

> I also feel hands-on learning is the best [way] for paraprofessionals to learn reference work. Currently we hold nine sessions conducted by reference librarians. I would like to see it expanded and have a part of the sessions held online, discovering our electronic resources and having them work at the reference desk with an assigned buddy to aid in the staff members' development. I also find it is important for staff to partake in webinars and to learn as much as possible about our electronic resources.

Assisting staff to better serve customers remains high on her dream list. The need to be empathetic and understand how best to assist customers brings a desire to focus on issues of diversity in workplace learning and performance programs: "Understanding that when a child has ADD he will need more understanding than the normal ('I've got a lot of energy to burn') child. Or if an adult is a slow learner, it will take more patience on your part to ensure this adult gets the information she is looking for. It is knowing these differences exist and how to cope with them in another venue that staff need instruction about."

"Learning is not a one-time event," Vaughn concludes. "It is a part of your life. If you quit learning, you quit living!"

When Sandra Smith dreams, those dreams begin with visions of budgets to pay for substitute staff while members of permanent staff are given time to learn:

> This budget would also include time to train the substitutes! Also, I would hire or develop people to be able to use the vast world of

online learning tools to develop new products for our staff to [use in] learn[ing]. . . . The "tech savvy developers" would be able to spend their time keeping up with all the new tech that will be coming down the pike in the learning field. Also, I need more skilled face-to-face trainers who have the skills to deliver training either in person or via tech. And I want a kick-ass LMS, meaning money to make the vendor do it my way.

Creating budgets that support learning are also high on Pat Wagner's wish list:

I would [want to] be able to hire enough people so a considerable amount of everybody's time is spent learning, that everybody is a learner, that everybody is a teacher. Regardless of technology and the latest toys and the latest theories, we can stop and say, "This is something interesting. It is worth pursuing." This is very important to me, because in our little business we have two key values: that what we do needs to be of service to people, but we don't take on projects unless we're learning something new. That's true of myself, and it's also true of my husband. We don't pursue consulting and training projects if we're not going to get something out of them besides money.

Among the other items on Smith's wish list are resources for scholarships to allow staff members to attend educational opportunities ranging from single college courses to entire degree programs (including those leading to MLS degrees), workshops, and conferences—those places where so many of us learn so much and then spread the wealth both within and outside our formal worksites. Having resources to recognize staff in meaningful ways for succeeding in learning is equally important, she maintains. Certificates, mugs, and other trophies need to be replaced with other forms of encouragement and recognition.

For Smith, it comes back to a key issue: "the difficulties that trainers have in getting others to understand the value of what we do." After all, if we can't make that sale, who will?

THE PLEASURES OF TRAINING-TEACHING-LEARNING

Gather workplace learning and performance leaders together, and you will hear plenty of grumbling about lack of time, lack of contact with colleagues in other organizations, lack of resources to do all that has to be done, and plenty of other challenges that can seem to be overwhelming. At the end of the day, however, you will not hear many of us talk about wanting to do anything other than train, teach, learn, and promote learning.

"I love what I do," Catherine Vaughn says. "It is one of the best jobs a person can have. I work with so many wonderful staff, volunteers, and customers that if one person is having a not-so-good day, usually the next person is. I find great satisfaction when I see the person I have been working with 'get it.' Their eyes light up and they are so excited. The pay is not high, but the personal rewards are so many!"

In offering suggestions to others involved in or contemplating a similar career, she suggests remembering this: "You are being watched, so be on your game. Always be observing; you never know when you can use something to benefit your learning sessions. Keep the lines of communication open with other instructors and organizations. As time allows, read. Read books on leadership, facilitating techniques, your local news. Anything can become something."

Peter Bromberg also refers to the pleasures his work provides:

> I think anyone who is involved with the promotion or delivery of continuing education and staff development is a lucky person. It's an immensely satisfying role to play, to be able to help create an environment and opportunities for others to expand their knowledge and abilities. I think, for many of us, that pleasure of helping people enrich themselves is why we became librarians. The difference for staff development professionals is that they are focusing on helping staff rather than the public, or students, or whatever the core service population of the institution might be. . . . Our skills, temperament, and ability to think strategically position us well for the roll of formal and informal leaders in our organizations. We tend to be more neutral and balanced in terms of organizational politics and better able to communicate in ways that are technically accurate and solution-oriented. The skills that allow us to excel at creating effective lesson plans and learning experiences are the same skills that allow us to communicate effectively with people across the organizational chart and help them find common ground around a shared vision or ideal.

Jay Turner speaks effusively of being enamored of the opportunities a career in workplace learning and performance offers:

> What I see in my organization and . . . what I hear from other libraries—mostly, but not necessarily absolutely—is that we work in

a field where staff like to learn. Not everyone will be rushing to sign up for your classes, but I'm amazed at how much people enjoy their own development. When I've gone to general training conferences and seminars, I hear how difficult it can be to get people to attend classes or to do some type of independent study. That just hasn't been my experience. . . . The pleasure for me comes from seeing others wanting to learn.

Much of what appeals to him is reflected in what he offers those who learn from him, and he is explicit in his recommendations to other current and prospective learning leaders. "Train only that which people don't already know," he suggests as a starting point, then continues with other recommendations:

Empower your followers—learners, in our instance—to take charge of their development. There's always something in it for them, your learners, even if it is not readily apparent. Try to help your followers see that early, whether you're teaching a class or doing something heavy like assisting your administration with managing a major change. . . . Exercise extreme self-care, as one of my mentors put it to me several years ago. Trainers and leaders often burn the candle from both ends. You're no good to anyone as a puddle of wax.

Pat Wagner loves those all-important moments "when people start talking and listening to each other about concerns they have in the workplace. It's when people really step back and are learning from each other. That moment infuses a room with almost a special kind of light. They've lost their defensiveness. They've lost their boundaries. They, as my husband would say, are more interested in finding out the truth than being right."

That "aha" moment, Wagner says, is what provides "the greatest pleasure . . . when you see someone go, 'I got it,' and they go back and try it, and it works. . . . that's the best. That's the heroin of being a trainer. That's what keeps you coming back. I don't care whether they thank me or not; that's not what it's about."

Those same moments help to motivate Louise Whitaker: "When I am working with staff, either in a formal setting or just wandering by their desk, and I can answer a question or teach them a new skill, and I see that light bulb go off, that makes my day. Not to toot my own horn, but I think I am good at what I do. It is fun to come to work."

By this time, it should be no surprise to readers that what draws us all together is a love of training, teaching, and learning; those moments that most effectively show us that our efforts have a positive impact lasting far beyond any single moment itself; and the opportunity workplace learning and performance offers us as leaders and as learners to create, nurture, and help sustain the communities of learning that contribute to the continuance of all we have developed collaboratively. We may not always—or even often—see the fruit that grows from the seeds we plant, but we know that others will. With your collaboration, we look forward to contributing to even greater results in the months and years and decades ahead of us.

NOTES

1. Tony Bingham and Marcia Conner, *The New Social Learning: A Guide to Transforming Organizations through Social Media* (San Francisco: Berrett-Koehler, 2010); Richard Florida, *The Great Reset: How New Ways of Living and Working Drive Post-Crash Prosperity* (New York: HarperCollins, 2010); Clay Shirky, *Here Comes Everybody: The Power of Organizing without Organizations* (New York: Penguin Press, 2008); Don Tapscott and Anthony Williams, *Wikinomics: How Mass Collaboration Changes Everything* (New York: Penguin Group, 2006).

2. Ray Oldenburg, *The Great Good Place: Cafés, Coffee Shops, Bookstores, Bars, Hair Salons and the Other Hangouts at the Heart of a Community* (New York: Marlowe, 1989).

3. Pew Research Center, "Pew Internet and American Life Project," www.pew internet.org; Pew Research Center, "Millennials: A Portrait of Generation Next," http://pewresearch.org/millennials/.

4. New Media Consortium, "Horizon Reports," www.nmc.org/publications/horizon; Len Safko, *The Social Media Bible: Tactics, Tools, and Strategies for Business Success* (Hoboken: John Wiley and Sons, 2010).

5. ASTD, "SOS Success Stories by Category," www.astd.org/membership/Chapter Leadership/ChapterManagement/SOSbycategory.htm.

6. James Kouzes and Barry Posner, *The Leadership Challenge*, 4th ed. (San Francisco: John Wiley and Sons, 2007).

7. Everett Rogers, *Diffusion of Innovations*, 5th ed. (New York: Free Press, 2003); Chip and Dan Heath, *Switch: How to Change Things When Change Is Hard* (New York: Broadway Books, 2010).

8. Malcolm Knowles, Elwood Holton, and Richard Swanson, *The Adult Learner*, 6th ed. (Burlington, Vt.: Elsevier, 2005); Peter Senge, *The Fifth Discipline: The Art and Practice of the Learning Organization*, 2nd. ed. (New York: Doubleday, 2006).

9. Frans Johansson, *The Medici Effect: Breakthrough Insights at the Intersection of Ideas, Concepts, and Cultures* (Boston: Harvard Business School Press, 2004).

10. ALA, "The H. W. Wilson Library Staff Development Grant," www.ala.org/alaawards grants/awardsrecords/wilsongrant/wilsongrant.cfm.

EMPLOYEE LEARNING & DEVELOPMENT CURRICULUM
CHARLOTTE MECKLENBURG LIBRARY

The Employee Learning and Development Curriculum (also available at www.alaeditions.org/webextras) was created as a learning guide for staff of the Charlotte Mecklenburg Library and is based on the Management Training Program and Curriculum created by Julia Lanham of the Charlotte Mecklenburg Library.

Employee Learning & Development Curriculum

The Charlotte Mecklenburg Library recognizes that our employees are our most valuable resource. A well-trained staff is crucial to the success of the Library. The Charlotte Mecklenburg Library invests in the learning and development of all our employees.

The following Employee Learning & Development Curriculum is a comprehensive personal development program designed to assist employees in developing a foundation of core skills needed to succeed at the Library.

The following areas have been identified as key to employee success at the Library:

- Communication
- Customer Service
- Ethics & Values
- Knowledge of the Library
- Learning & Personal Growth
- Safety & Security
- Technology

The Library recognizes that competencies in these areas are critical to the success of staff and the Library. The course plan included here contains seven core classes which are required of all employees*. Following that is a list of elective courses that any Library employee may enroll in. All employees are encouraged to work with their supervisors and select at least two elective courses that meet their development needs. This plan is not intended to be the final or only resource staff should utilize when developing or strengthening their skills. Rather, these courses are a foundation upon which staff can develop and improve their own skills. All staff are encouraged to identify and utilize other training resources to grow and develop both personally and professionally.

All Library employees are required to participate in the Employee Learning & Development Program. New employees should follow the designated timeline described. Current employees may exercise flexibility in scheduling courses; however, all required training must be completed by December 31, 2010. Credit will be given for courses already completed. Failure to meet the required schedule could result in a negative impact on your performance rating.

All courses may require pre-work and post-work to help you learn the material. It is your responsibility to complete pre-work prior to attending a session. If you have not completed the pre-work, you may be asked to reschedule and attend training after completing the pre-work. Your training record will show that you have completed a course once the post-work has been received and evaluated.

Courses are offered through the Library and Mecklenburg County. Periodically, courses will be reviewed for relevancy and may be modified to include new ideas, processes, or resources.

Courses are offered through a variety of methods including: face-to-face, online asynchronous (self-paced), online synchronous (live), or blended (combination of these methods).

*Diversity Competency Development and Non-Violent Crisis Intervention are strongly recommended but not required for part-time staff.

Employee Learning & Development Schedule

- **Within first week of employment with the Library, you should have enrolled in and/or completed the following courses:**

  New Employee Orientation

  Library Safety & Security Orientation

- **Within 6 months after you begin employment with the Library, you should have enrolled in and/or completed the following course:**

  Customer Service

- **Within 12 months after you begin employment with the Library, you should have enrolled in and/or completed the following courses:**

  Diversity Competency Development*

  Ethics

  Non-Violent Crisis Intervention*

  Sexual Harassment

*Diversity Competency Development and Non-Violent Crisis Intervention are strongly recommended but not required for part-time staff.

Training Policies

Registration
To register for both Library and Mecklenburg County Courses, look for the "Training and Development" tab in myHR. Note that some courses require that you complete other courses before you can register. If you need assistance, please contact a member of the Human Resources Department or e-mail **learning@plcmc.org**.

Cancelling/Rescheduling Training
To cancel or reschedule your registration, contact the Mecklenburg County Employee Services Center by phone at **704.432.myHR (6947)** or by e-mail **Helpdesk.MyHR@mecklenburgcountync.gov**. Include in your communication your name, employee ID number (which can be found on your ID badge), as well as the name of the class you need to cancel. If you do not cancel your registration at least 24 hours in advance of the course and do not attend training, you will be marked as a "no show" and an automatic notice will be issued to you and your supervisor announcing a charge for your course registration. The Library also may be charged a "No Show" fee (see below).

Attendance Policy
Please note that when you register for a class, you are expected to attend. Mecklenburg County charges a $25 no-show fee for their training courses (different costs may apply to certain courses.) The Library must absorb this cost. The Library does not charge for its courses (designated by the course code LIB) unless otherwise noted. Frequent no shows to training courses could result in disciplinary action against the employee; therefore, we ask that you make every effort possible to attend. If the course is full and others are waitlisted, your failure to attend has kept someone else from attending and benefiting from the course.

Tracking Your Progress

Use this chart to track your progress on completing the required courses. Your manager or supervisor as well as Human Resources will also track your course completions. You may contact us at any time regarding the courses you've completed.

Required Courses	Date Registered	Date Completed
LIB001 New Employee Orientation		
LIB035 Library Safety & Security Orientation		
LIB036 Customer Service		
DIV101 Diversity Competency Development*		
coming soon from Mecklenburg County Ethics		
LIB017 Non-Violent Crisis Intervention*		
LIB038 Sexual Harassment		
Supplemental Courses (choose at least 2)	Date Registered	Date Completed
LIB030 or M4R120 Basics of Training Design		
LIB039 Information Assistance		
LIB040 Merchandising the Collection		
M4R104 Presentation Skills		
LIB048 Programming for Teens		
LIB008 Readers Advisory Basics		
LIB010 Readers Advisory for Teens and Adults		
LIB009 Readers Advisory for Youth		
LIB044 Volunteer Management		
LIB043 Volunteers at PLCMC		
LIB046 Working with Teens		

*Diversity Competency Development Training and Non-Violent Crisis Intervention are strongly recommended but not required for part-time staff.

Have questions about the program or courses?

Please contact the Learning & Development Coordinator at **704.416.0454** or by e-mail **learning@plcmc.org**.

COURSE CATALOG REQUIRED COURSES

Required Course *related competency*	Course Description	Course Length	Recommended Completion Date	Course Delivery Method	Course Sponsor
New Employee Orientation **LIB001** Customer Service, Ethics & Values, Knowledge of the Library	For all new Library employees. Learn about the organization, values, mission & vision, leadership, team, functional areas, policies & procedures, resources, etc. After completing this course, you will be able to: • State the vision and mission of the Charlotte Mecklenburg Library • Describe the organizational structure of the Library • Know where to look for information about benefits at the Library • Register for training • Cancel or reschedule training	3 hrs	First week of employment (Current employees are encouraged to complete the new, self-paced online session)	Face-to-Face Beginning 1/1/2010 this will be offered online	Library
Library Safety & Security Orientation **LIB035** (Knowledge of the Library, Safety & Security)	The safety of library staff and the public is our number one priority at all times. In this self-paced online tutorial, you will learn the basic security policies and procedures of the Charlotte Mecklenburg Library. After completing this course, you will be able to: • Identify where to find Library rules and regulations • Describe the procedure for handling a disruptive customer • Know how and when to enter a potential problem and incident report • Describe what to do if you lose your key and/or security badge • Know basic security procedures for entering, leaving, and occupying the library • Know how to call and/or page Security • Describe Code Adam/Amber procedures • Describe what to do in a medical emergency • Describe what to do when a fire alarm goes off • Describe what to do in severe weather • Describe what to do in a power outage • Describe what to do during a bomb threat	TBD	First week of employment and annually thereafter	Beginning 1/1/2010 this will be offered online	Library

COURSE CATALOG REQUIRED COURSES

Required Course *related competency*	Course Description	Course Length	Recommended Completion Date	Course Delivery Method	Course Sponsor
Non-Violent Crisis Intervention LIB017 Communication, Customer Service, Safety & Security	Non-Violent Crisis Intervention is a highly interactive 2-day workshop that equips staff with techniques necessary to deal with aggressive customers in a safe manner. After completing this course, you will be able to: • Illustrate how personal space affects the anxiety level of an individual. • Portray how body posture and motion affects the anxiety level of an individual. • Demonstrate how inappropriate staff reaction can cause an escalation in behavior • Provide the best possible care, welfare, safety, and security for individuals in our facilities • Understand the causes of fear • Learn how to make fear/anxiety work for you in a crisis situation. • Build confidence in your ability to keep yourself and others safe in a crisis situation. • Maintain professional attitudes during a crisis intervention by rational detaching. • Foster an awareness of the fact that how a verbal statement is delivered is equally, if not more important, than the actual words used. *This course is strongly recommended but not required for part-time staff.	16 hrs	0-12 months of employment and must be recertified on an annual basis afterward	Face-to-face	Library

COURSE CATALOG REQUIRED COURSES

Required Course related competency	Course Description	Course Length	Recommended Completion Date	Course Delivery Method	Course Sponsor
Customer Service LIB036 Communication, Customer Service	Customer Service training at the Library will provide you with the skills and knowledge to be responsive and effective in addressing internal and external customer needs while understanding the impact of customer interactions on organizational success. After completing this course, you will be able to: • Compare and contrast customer-focused service with staff-focused service • Explain why an internal customer request is as important as an external customer request • Employ interaction techniques to handle any request right the first time • List key phrases to adopt and avoid when dealing with customers • Describe techniques to diffuse the upset/complaining/angry customers • Operate using the concepts of team based customer service	4 hrs	0-6 months of employment	Face-to-face	Library
Ethics Communication, Ethics & Values	This course is currently being developed by Mecklenburg County to be implemented in fall 2009. More information will come as soon as we have the details.	TBD	0-12 months of employment	Face-to-face	Mecklenburg County
Sexual Harassment LIB038 Communication	Prevention is the best tool to eliminate sexual harassment in the workplace. After completing this course, you will be able to: • Define sexual harassment • Recognize sexual harassment • Explain what your role as an employee is to stop sexual harassment • Explain what your responsibilities are as an employee regarding sexual harassment	2 hrs	0-12 months of employment	Beginning in fall 2009 this will be offered online	Library

COURSE CATALOG REQUIRED COURSES

Required Course *related competency*	Course Description	Course Length	Recommended Completion Date	Course Delivery Method	Course Sponsor
Diversity Competency Development **DIV101** Communication	This is a required workshop for all County employees and provides hands-on experience where participants will learn how to better manage "cultural collisions" routinely encountered in a large organization. Highlights include: • Awareness and assessment of one's own values, experiences, and perceptions of others • Looking beyond obvious differences to find the similarities in people • Learning how to understand the viewpoints, norms and styles of others • Addressing culturally biased behaviors to resolve conflict, solve problems and increase performance • Recognize the positive value and productive contributions of people with different backgrounds and perspectives • Communicating effectively with people of different cultures, backgrounds and perspectives To better understand the Diversity Management Plans for Mecklenburg County, visit *Diversity In Mecklenburg County* at http://www.charmeck.org and click on *Diversity Management Plan* on the left of the page. *This course is strongly recommended but not required for part-time staff.	7 hrs	0-12 months of employment	Face-to-face	Mecklenburg County

COURSE CATALOG SUPPLEMENTAL COURSES

Supplemental Course *related competency*	Course Description	Course Length	Recommended for	Course Delivery Method	Course Sponsor
Basics of Training Design LIB030 or M4R120 Communication, Learning & Personal Growth	If you design training programs, this class can get you on the right track to an effective design of learning opportunities. After completing this course, you will be able to: • Develop strategies which are learner-focused and incorporate effective training methods and styles • Define the characteristics of and importance of understanding the Adult Learner • Define the 80/20 rule, Pikes Law, Howells Levels of Competence and how they influence training design • Develop training objectives and desired outcomes • Practice using skills in developing training modules	4 hrs	Recommended for staff who design public or staff training.	Face-to-face	Library or Mecklenburg County
Information Assistance LIB039 Communication, Customer Service, Information Retrieval	Learn the basics of the reference interview and connecting customers to the information they need. By the end of the workshop, you will be able to: • Demonstrate three models of reference behaviors • Name three strategies in conducting a reference transaction with a child • Give three tips on handling a reference interview with multiple patrons, an angry patron, an ESL patron, and/or a hearing impaired patron • Describe three criteria in evaluating a reference source	2 hrs	Recommended for all staff.	Face-to-face	Library

COURSE CATALOG SUPPLEMENTAL COURSES

Supplemental Course *related competency*	Course Description	Course Length	Recommended for	Course Delivery Method	Course Sponsor
Merchandising the Collection **LIB040** Customer Service, Programming	Merchandising the collection is essential to a customer-focused environment where materials are easy to find. In this session, you will learn to merchandise library materials in the branch so the displays help to circulate materials and can be replenished quickly. After completing this course, you will be able to: • List the desired outcomes of well-merchandised collections in a library environment. • Describe how merchandising plays a role in enhancing the customer experience. • Describe the elements that make an effective display. • List the selection techniques for choosing materials for a display. • Describe the elements of effective signage. • Develop ideas for successful merchandising of collections in the library.	2 hrs	Recommended for all staff who create displays. It is suggested that each location send at least one staff member to this course.	Face-to-face	Library
Presentation Skills **M4R104** Communication, Learning & Personal Growth	The #1 fear is public speaking! The best way to overcome this fear is by being prepared. This workshop will provide tips and tools to overcome fear and will cover the basics in how to prepare and deliver an effective presentation. This workshop is for those who are serious about improving their delivery skills. Participants will be given an opportunity to apply this information by making a short presentation on the second day of class. Polish your skills with the help of experienced public speaking coaches. After completing this course, you will be able to: • Address the fears around speaking before others. • Develop a plan/script to use in preparing for your presentation. • Determine effective visual aids to use in a presentation. • Prepare for delivering an effective presentation.	12 hrs	Recommended for all staff who give presentations or who would like to learn to give presentations.	Face-to-face	Library or Mecklenburg County

COURSE CATALOG SUPPLEMENTAL COURSES

Supplemental Course *related competency*	Course Description	Course Length	Recommended for	Course Delivery Method	Course Sponsor
Programming for Teens **LIB048** Customer Service, Programming	Learn how to plan, implement, and market programs in unique ways that are attractive and welcoming to teens. After completing this course, you will be able to: • Discuss why teen programming in the library is important • Identify elements needed in effective teen programming • Find unique program ideas • List strategies to get teens involved • Market programs effectively to teens	2 hrs	All staff who work with teen programming or who want to learn about programming for teens.	Face-to-face	Library
(RA) Readers Advisory Basics **LIB008** Communication, Customer Service, Information Retrieval, Reader's Advisory	Learn how to connect Library customers of any age with books using basic reader's advisory concepts. After completing this course, you will be able to: • Identify the elements of appeal or gateways into fiction • Conduct a reader's advisory interview • Discuss major genres and popular authors in adult, young adult, and children's fiction • Discuss at least two innovations in reader's advisory services	2 hrs	Recommended for all new library experiences staff and other staff who want to learn or refresh their reader's advisory skills.	Face-to-Face Beginning 1/1/2010 this will be offered online	Library
(RA) Resources for Adults & YA **LIB010** Communication, Customer Service, Information Retrieval, Reader's Advisory	In this follow-up session to Reader's Advisory Basics, you will learn the major electronic and print resources used for reader's advisory with teens and adults. After completing this course, you will be able to: • Select an appropriate resource to use in answering a reader's advisory question from an adult or young adult. • Complete a basic search in NoveList and at least two other online resources/databases to answer an adult and a young adult reader's advisory question. • Use at least two books or other written materials to provide reader's advisory to adults and young adults.	2 hrs	Recommended for all new library experiences staff and other staff who want to learn or refresh their reader's advisory skills.	Face-to-Face Beginning 1/1/2010 this will be offered online	Library

COURSE CATALOG SUPPLEMENTAL COURSES

Supplemental Course *related competency*	Course Description	Course Length	Recommended for	Course Delivery Method	Course Sponsor
(RA) Resources for Children **LIB009** Communication, Customer Service, Information Retrieval, Reader's Advisory	In this follow-up session to Reader's Advisory Basics, you will learn the major electronic and print resources used for reader's advisory with children infants to age 12 and their caregivers. After completing this course, you will be able to: • Select an appropriate resource to use in answering a reader's advisory question from a child or caregiver. • Complete a basic search in NoveList and at least two other online resources/databases to answer a children's reader's advisory question. • Use at least two books or other written materials to answer a children's reader's advisory question.	2 hrs	Recommended for all new library experiences staff and other staff who want to learn or refresh their reader's advisory skills.	Face-to-Face Beginning 1/1/2010 this will be offered online	Library
Volunteer Management **LIB044** Communication, Knowledge of the Library, Learning & Personal Growth	Our vision is to create a model volunteer program for the Library. A successful volunteer effort will allow the Library to address needs and leverage library resources in ways that we cannot now imagine. After completing this course, you will be able to: • Describe why we need volunteers and how volunteers help the Library • Describe the motivation and rights of volunteers • Describe the process of volunteer recruitment: advertising, background checks, extending an offer, training volunteers • List the communication ideals when working with volunteers • Address performance problems with a volunteer • Describe the boundaries of the employee/volunteer relationship	2 hrs	Recommended for all staff who manage or supervise volunteers	Face-to-Face Beginning 1/1/2010 this will be offered online	Library

COURSE CATALOG SUPPLEMENTAL COURSES

Supplemental Course *related competency*	Course Description	Course Length	Recommended for	Course Delivery Method	Course Sponsor
Volunteers at the Library **LIB043** Communication, Knowledge of the Library, Learning & Personal Growth	This training session is designed to help all staff members work successfully with volunteers. An effective volunteer program requires cooperation between staff and volunteers and a commitment from both to encourage and respect the contributions of the other. After completing this course, you will be able to: • Identify ways to increase staff participation and effectiveness with the volunteer program • Describe the elements that make up a good volunteer experience • Explain the Library volunteer philosophy • Locate the staff volunteer handbook which will detail policies and procedures for working with and managing volunteers	2 hrs	Recommended for all staff who work with volunteers or would like to find out how they can utilize volunteers in their department.	Face-to-Face Beginning 1/1/2010 this will be offered online	Library
Working with Teens **LIB046** Communication, Customer Service, Programming	This Ain't Your Mama's Library!: Creating a New Generation of Library Services for a New Generation of Library Users In this session, we will cover brain research and adolescent behavior, stages/milestones of adolescence, developmental needs of teens, 40 developmental assets, tying it all together to best serve teens After completing this course, you will be able to: • Explain the connections between youth development and library services • Apply new information about adolescent brain development to serving young adults in libraries • Deliver quality reference services for young adults • Develop ideas for successful interactions with young adults in the library	3 hrs	Recommended for all Library Experiences staff but especially those staff who interact with teens.	Face-to-face	Library

BIBLIOGRAPHY

Bennis, Warren. *On Becoming a Leader.* Reading: Addison-Wesley, 1989.

Biech, Elaine. *Training for Dummies.* Hoboken: Wiley, 2005.

———, ed. *The ASTD Handbook for Workplace Learning Professionals.* Alexandria: ASTD Press, 2008.

Bingham, Tony, and Marcia Conner. *The New Social Learning: A Guide to Transforming Organizations through Social Media.* San Francisco: Berrett-Koehler, 2010.

Block, Peter. *Flawless Consulting: A Guide to Getting Your Expertise Used.* 2nd ed. San Francisco: Jossey-Bass/Pfeiffer, 2000.

Blowers, Helene, and Lori Reed. "The C's of Our Sea Change: Plans for Training Staff, from Core Competencies to LEARNING 2.0." *Computers in Libraries,* February 2007, 14–15.

Brinkerhoff, Robert O. *Telling Training's Story: Evaluation Made Simple, Credible, and Effective.* San Francisco: Berrett-Koehler, 2006.

Bromberg, Peter. "New Jersey's Train-the-Trainer: Creating a Community of Library Instructors." South Jersey Regional Library Cooperative website, 2004, www.sjrlc.org/ttt.htm.

Coleman, Maurice. "5 Tips for Trainers to Prevent TechFail." *ALA Learning,* http://alalearning.org/2010/02/04/5-tips-for-trainers-to-prevent-techfail/.

"Creating the 4th Place: A Community Gathering Place for (Social) Learning." *T Is for Training,* episode 53, http://tisfortraining .wordpress.com/2010/08/13/t-is-for-training-53-creating-the-4th -place-a-community-gathering-place-for-social-learning.

Davidson, Jeffrey. *The Complete Idiot's Guide to Change Management.* Indianapolis: Alpha, 2002.

DeNoon, Daniel. "Fear of Public Speaking Hardwired." *WebMD,* April 20, 2006, www.webmd.com/anxiety-panic/guide/20061101/ fear-public-speaking.

Dirkx, John. "The Power of Feelings: Emotion, Imagination, and the Construction of Meaning in Adult Learning." *New Directions for Adult and Continuing Education: The New Update on Adult Learning Theory* 89 (2001): 68.

Florida, Richard. *The Great Reset: How New Ways of Living and Working Drive Post-Crash Prosperity.* New York: HarperCollins, 2010.

Giesecke, Joan, and Beth McNeil. *Fundamentals of Library Supervision.* Chicago: American Library Association, 2005.

Gladwell, Malcolm. *The Tipping Point: How Little Things Can Make a Big Difference.* New York: Little, Brown, 2000.

Greenleaf, Robert. *Servant Leadership: A Journey into the Nature of Legitimate Power and Greatness.* New York: Paulist Press, 1977.

Heath, Chip, and Dan Heath. *Switch: How to Change Things When Change Is Hard.* New York: Broadway Books, 2010.

Hurst-Wahl, Jill. "Community, Collaboration, and Learning: Time for the Fourth Place." *Digitization 101*, August 17, 2010, http://hurstassociates.blogspot.com.

Hyman, Karen. "Customer Service and the 'Rule of 1965.'" *American Libraries*, 30, no. 9 (1999): 54–56.

Jefferson, Andrew, Roy Pollock, and Calhoun Wick. *Getting Your Money's Worth from Training and Development: A Guide to Breakthrough Learning for Managers.* San Francisco: Pfeiffer: An Imprint of Wiley, 2009.

Johansson, Frans. *The Medici Effect: Breakthrough Insights at the Intersection of Ideas, Concepts, and Cultures.* Boston: Harvard Business School Press, 2004.

Kirkpatrick, Donald, and James Kirkpatrick. *Evaluating Training Programs: The Four Levels.* San Francisco: Berrett-Koehler, 2006.

Knowles, Malcolm, Elwood Holton, and Richard Swanson. *The Adult Learner*, 6th ed. Burlington, Vt.: Elsevier, 2005.

Kouzes, James, and Barry Posner. *The Leadership Challenge*, 4th ed. San Francisco: John Wiley and Sons, 2007.

Lippitt, Gordon, and Ronald Lippitt. *The Consulting Process in Action*, 2nd ed. San Diego: University Associates, 1986.

Masters, Ann. "CLENE History." *ALA Learning*, December 2006, http://alalearning.org/about/history-of-the-learning-round-table.

New Media Consortium. "Horizon Reports." www.nmc.org/publications/horizon.

Oldenburg, Ray. *The Great Good Place: Cafés, Coffee Shops, Bookstores, Bars, Hair Salons and Other Hangouts at the Heart of a Community.* New York: Marlowe, 1989.

Patterson, Kerry, Joseph Grenny, Ron McMillan, and Al Switzler. *Crucial Conversations: Tools for Talking When Stakes Are High.* New York: McGraw-Hill, 2002.

Pew Research Center. "Millennials: A Portrait of Generation Next," http://pewresearch.org/millennials/.

———. "Pew Internet and American Life Project," www.pewinternet.org.

Rogers, Everett. *The Diffusion of Innovations*, 5th ed. New York: Free Press, 2003.

Ruark, Benjamin. "The Year 2013: ARDDIE Is In, ADDIE Is Out." *T+D* 62, no. 7 (2008): 44–49, http://findarticles.com/p/articles/mi_m4467/is_200807/ai_n27996027/.

Rubin, Rhea Joyce. *Demonstrating Results: Using Outcome Measurement in Your Library.* Chicago: American Library Association, 2006.

Safko, Len. *The Social Media Bible: Tactics, Tools, and Strategies for Business Success.* Hoboken: John Wiley and Sons, 2010.

Senge, Peter. *The Fifth Discipline: The Art and Practice of the Learning Organization*, 2nd. ed. New York: Doubleday, 2006.

Shelton, Charlotte, Mindi McKenna, and John Darling. "Leading in the Age of Paradox: Optimizing Behavioral Style, Job Fit and Cultural Cohesion." *Leadership and Organization Development Journal* 23, no. 7 (2002): 372–379.

Shirky, Clay. *Here Comes Everybody: The Power of Organizing without Organizations.* New York: Penguin Press, 2008.

Signorelli, Paul. "Community, Collaboration, and Learning: Time for the Fourth Place." *Building Creative Bridges*, August 15, 2010, http://buildingcreative bridges.wordpress.com/2010/08/15/community-collaboration-and-learning-time-for-the-fourth-place.

———. "Dynamic Web Conferencing and Presentation Skills for Effective Meetings, Trainings, and Learning Sessions." http://paulsignorelli.com/PDFs/Bibliography--Webconferencing_Resources.pdf.

———. "E-learning, Google Chat, and Innovation." *Building Creative Bridges*, http://buildingcreativebridges.wordpress.com/2010/01/13/e-learning-google-chat-and-innovation/.

————. "E-learning: Annotated Bibliography for Library Training Programs." http://paulsignorelli.com/PDFs/E-learning_Annotated_ Bibliography_June_2009.pdf.

————. "Skype and Low-Cost E-learning Delivered at the Moment of Need." *Building Creative Bridges*, http://buildingcreativebridges. wordpress.com/2010/01/22/skype-and-low-cost-e-learning-delivered -at-the-moment-of-need/.

Stephens, Michael. "PLA Learning 2.0 Presentation." www.slideshare.net/ mstephens7/pla-learning-20- presentation.

————, and Warren Cheetham. "The Impact of Learning 2.0 Programs in Australian Libraries," http://research.tametheweb.com.

Tapscott, Don, and Anthony Williams. *Wikinomics: How Mass Collaboration Changes Everything.* New York: Penguin Group, 2006.

Weiss, Alan. *Million Dollar Consulting: The Professional's Guide to Growing a Practice,* 3rd ed. New York: McGraw-Hill, 2003.

Whitworth, Laura, Henry Kimsey-House, and Phil Sandhahl. *Co-Active Coaching: New Skills for Coaching People toward Success in Work and Life.* Mountain View, Calif.: Davies-Black, 2007.

Wick, Calhoun W., Roy V. H. Pollock, Andrew McK. Jefferson, and Richard D. Flanagan. *The Six Disciplines of Breakthrough Learning: How to Turn Training and Development into Business Results.* San Francisco: Pfeiffer, 2006.

INDEX

INDEX

INDEX

You may also be interested in

ORGANIZATIONAL STORYTELLING FOR LIBRARIANS
USING STORIES FOR EFFECTIVE LEADERSHIP
Kate Marek

Just as literature often enhances learning, the power of storytelling can be very effective when applied to leadership and management. Marek provides the tools and explains the process of successful organizational storytelling.

PRINT ISBN: 978-0-8389-1079-5
120 PAGES / 6" X 9"

CAREER DEVELOPMENT

WHAT THEY DON'T TEACH YOU IN LIBRARY SCHOOL
ELISABETH DOUCETT
ISBN: 978-0-8389-3592-7

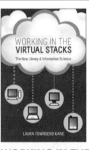

WORKING IN THE VIRTUAL STACKS
EDITED BY LAURA TOWNSEND KANE
ISBN: 978-0-8389-1103-7

HOW TO STAY AFLO. THE ACADEMIC LIBR JOB POOL
EDITED BY TERESA Y. NE
FOREWORD BY CAMILA .
ISBN: 978-0-8389-1080-1

ADMINISTRATION & MANAGEMENT

COACHING IN THE LIBRARY, 2E
RUTH F. METZ
ISBN: 978-0-8389-1037-5

BE A GREAT BOSS
CATHERINE HAKALA-AUSPERK
ISBN: 978-0-8389-1068-9

DEALING WITH DIFFICULT PEOPLE IN THE LIBRARY, 2E
MARK R. WILLIS
ISBN: 978-0-8389-1114-3

Order today at **alastore.ala.org** or **866-746-7252!**
ALA Store purchases fund advocacy, awareness, and accreditation programs for library professionals worldwide.